THE CASS PROP....

Armageddon Approaches

by Ian Gurney

The Bible's Greatest Secret
Revealed - **Judgement Day**

IGP
1999, 2001   IAN GURNEY

And he said, Verily I say unto you, No prophet is accepted in his own country.

Luke 4. verse 24

In Classic Greek Mythology, Cassandra, the daughter of King Priam and Hecuba, was granted the power of prophecy by Apollo. However, when she refused Apollo's advances, he decreed that she would always prophecy truthfully, but would never be believed in her own land.

First published in 1999 by IGP
Revised edition published in 2001 by IGP
All rights reserved.

A catalogue record for this book is available from the Library of Congress.

Cover idea by Ian Gurney.

Cover photograph courtesy of U.S. Dept. of Energy.

Printed in the United States by AlphaGraphics.

ISBN 0 9535813 1 4. 2nd revised and enlarged edition
(ISBN 0 9535813 0 6. 1st edition)

For further information www.caspro.com

This book is dedicated to Joanne Slater, without whose help it would not have been possible.

With love and many thanks,
Ian.

The Cassandra Prophecy

There is no power representing the good or the just……. Power, whomsoever exercises it, is the Devil, the corruptor of Man.

Thucydedes 431 BC

Introduction

Now I am come to make thee understand what shall befall thy people in the latter days.
Daniel 10. verse14

There are those who believe in the gift of prophecy, those who are unsure and those who do not believe. However, each and every one of us is curious about the future, particularly our own. I am not a prophet, what I have tried to do in the following pages is to interpret ancient prophecies and compare them with events that are happening now.

I have also, through research and simple arithmetic discovered the Bible's greatest secret, Judgement Day. A secret that has remained because academics and theologians have through the years, compounded an error concerning the mistaken identification of a major event in religious history.

First however, it is important to understand what kind of people the prophets were, what they understood of the world, how their minds worked. The Biblical prophets in particular, ranging from approximately 600 BC until 70 AD were in terms of twentieth century knowledge and understanding, very simple people. This is in no way meant to deride them or to be disrespectful, it is a simple fact. Daniel for instance, received his visions around the middle of the sixth century BC. What would he or any of his contemporaries know of tank battles, aerial warfare, missiles, attack helicopters, space travel or any of the other technological developments that we take for granted as the twentieth century draws to a close.

Yet the prophets were aware of the great importance of communicating the visions they had seen so that they could be understood in the future. As I said, these were simple men but very devout and intelligent. In order to be understood they used similes, comparing those things around them that they knew and understood and likening them to the events they had seen in their visions.

Imagine seeing visions of modern warfare over two thousand years ago. You would have no idea of the machinery and destruction caused by the weaponry of the late twentieth century and yet a description of the vision has to be given. Consider then, the following verse:

A fire devoureth before them; and behind them a flame burneth: the land is as the garden of Eden before them, and behind them a desolate wilderness; yes, and nothing shall escape them.
Joel 2. verse 3

Here, Joel is describing a vision he sees five hundred years before the birth of Jesus Christ. He could at that time have had no idea of modern warfare, but by using similes and his descriptive powers he shows us a graphic scenario of twentieth century war.

Not one of the ancient prophets could have fully understood the world in the final years of the twentieth century. Even Nostradamus writing in the sixteenth century, though far more informed and knowledgeable than the Biblical prophets, could not have fully grasped the inventions and technology of our world. He too uses his descriptive powers and similes to convey his message.

De nuict soleil penseront avoir veu,
Quand le pourceau demi-homme on verra:
Bruict, chant, bataille, au ciel battre aperceu:
Et bestes brutes a parler lon orra.

At night they will think they have seen the sun,
When they see the half pig man:
Noise, screams, battles seen fought in the skies,
And the brute beasts will be heard to speak.
Century 1. Quatrain 64

A prophet's credibility is often difficult to establish, but Nostradamus is an exception. Here he is giving a perfect description of aerial warfare. The simile "half pig man" refers to the profile of a pilot wearing his flying helmet, his oxygen mask giving him a snout like a pig. The last line seems to be Nostradamus' description of radio communication between the pilots. In the first chapter there are more examples of the fulfilled prophecies of Nostradamus, as well as brief descriptions of the main prophets interpreted in this book.

Perhaps one of the most interesting conclusions about the prophecies set out in this book, is that it appears that the true interpretation of them has only been possible in the latter half of the 20th. Century. The datings in the forthcoming chapter, Judgement Day, relate directly to events that have only occurred over the last fifty five years, therefore making redundant any interpretations of the prophecies, be it The Bible or Nostradamus, that appeared before this time. It is therefore possible to surmise that the prophecies that have been handed down to mankind over the centuries where only meant to be understood when that time actually arrived. That time appears to be now.

Paracelsus, the Swiss physician and seer describes this idea in a convoluted but extremely succint way in the Twenty Sixth Magic Figure of his prognostications.

For when the time cometh, also therewith cometh that wherefore the time hath come.

It seems that despite many attempts to interpret the ancient prophecies over the centuries, mankind has failed to do so correctly because all the events and situations where not in place. It is only now, at the beginning of the twenty first century, that it is possible to reveal the true meanings contained within prophecy, and there is only one conclusion we can reach with regard to this fact. The time is at hand.

*So likewise ye, when ye shall see all these things,
know that it is near, even at the doors.*

St. Mathew 24. verse 33

I have written this book as honestly as I can, with no bias. I have attempted at all times during my research and writing to keep an open mind on the subject and be non judgmental. I express no opinions, merely trying to interpret the messages contained in the ancient prophecies as clearly and correctly as possible. It would seem that if my interpretations are correct we are about to face the greatest calamity that mankind has ever experienced. If you are curious about your future, read on.

Chapter 1
The Prophets and the Prophecies

But the day of the Lord will come as a thief in the night.

2nd Peter 3. verse 10

The Bible is probably the most important book in the world. Contained within its pages is not only the history of the world up to the present day, but the future of the world, with precise datings up to the reappearance of the Son of Man on Earth.

For as the lightning cometh out of the east, and shineth even unto the west; so shall also the coming of the Son of man be.

Mathew 24. verse 27

In the course of this book I will show how Daniel the Old Testament prophet, was shown visions some 2,500 years ago, that correctly predicted Alexander the Great's defeat of the Persian Empire, the huge strength of the Roman Empire and the rise of Islam, together with precise datings for the Arab-Israeli six day war, the Camp David Agreement and the year that God will establish His Kingdom on earth - Judgement Day.

Once again we have to understand what Daniel knew of the world around him. The Book of Daniel begins with a very precise dating.

In the third year of the reign of Jehoiakim King of Judah came Nebuchadnezzar King of Babylon unto Jerusalem, and besieged it.

Daniel 1. verse 1

History is fairly precise with its datings concerning Nebuchadnezzar. He came to power in Babylon in 605 BC and his army besieged Jerusalem in 598 BC, finally destroying the city and the Temple in 586 BC. Those that were left alive of the House of Judah, of which Daniel was one, were deported to Babylon.

Daniel would have been well aware of the history of the Houses of Judah and Israel. The Exodus from Egypt under Moses is dated at 1290 BC, culminating after 40 years in the wilderness with the defeat of Palestine in 1250 BC when Joshua fought the Battle of Jericho.

Between 1005 BC and 925 BC Jerusalem, ruled over by King David and King Solomon, was a sanctuary, but between 925 BC and 722 BC Israel and Judah divided, ending with the capture of Samaria by Sargon II and the deportation of Israel to Nineveh in 722 BC. In 625 BC the Neo-Babylonian or Chaldean Empire rose to power and destroyed Ninevah in 612 BC. Then came Nebuchadnezzar in 605 BC.

Chapter 8 of the Book of Daniel is among the most fascinating chapters in the Bible. In it the reader is given 3 specific dates; of these dates two are not in doubt, but the third date, given in an obscure way, has never until now been correctly translated. The same can be said of Chapter 12 of Daniel. In this chapter two precise numbers are given in the same obscure way and a starting date is also given, by which a simple arithmetic addition gives us the year of Judgement Day. However, for over a thousand years scholars and theologians have incorrectly interpreted the starting date. In the next chapter I will show the reader how a simple mistake and a misunderstood interpretation have kept hidden one of the greatest mysteries of the Bible.

If the Book of Daniel is the Old Testament's greatest book of prophecy, then the New Testament's greatest prophetic book is the Revelation, the final book of the Bible. Revelation was written in the first century AD, around the time that Jerusalem was being attacked and destroyed by the Romans under Titus Andronicus, son of Emperor Vespasius in 70 AD.

It was written by St. John the Divine after his banishment from Ephesus now in modern day Turkey, for preaching the gospel of Jesus Christ.

I John, who also am your brother, and companion in tribulation, and in the Kingdom and patience of Jesus Christ, was in the isle that is called Patmos, for the word of God and the testimony of Jesus Christ.

Revelation 1. verse 8

Patmos is in the Greek Dodecanese islands, just off the coast of western Turkey. St. John received the Revelation whilst sheltering in a cave now known as the Sacred Cave. Visitors to Patmos, designated a Holy island under Greek law in 1988 will find the Sacred Cave surrounded by a small beautiful 11th century church, halfway up the winding road between the port or Skala and the hilltop village or Chora. Inside the Sacred Cave, adorned with religious artefacts, there are two marks, one on the floor of the cave the other on the cave wall. Both these marks are surrounded by a silver halo marking the place where St John lay his head and where the angel stood whilst St John received the vision of the Revelation.

The church of St John the Divine dominates the hilltop town and is surrounded by a medieval fortress. Inside its treasury are some of the most beautiful and striking religious artefacts in Europe or Asia, including a superb library of the scriptures and everywhere you look are murals, mosaics and pictures of Ioannes Theologus - St John the Divine.

The visions that John received were of the future. In the visions he sees the rise to power of the Holy Roman Empire, culminating in the Europe of the 20th century. He is given the secrets of the last seven plagues, the rise of the final antichrist, the fall of the Church and the final judgement. Revelation also gives precise datings for the rebirth of the state of Israel in 1948. Once again though, scholars and theologians have been unable or unwilling to translate these dates correctly due to two simple mistakes that have been made in the interpretations of Daniel, and in the chapter Judgement Day these mistakes will be identified and rectified, giving the reader a clear and frightening scenario of the future.

> *Bestes farouches de faim fleuves tranner,*
> *Plus part du champ encontre Hister sera.*
> *En caige de fer le grand fera treisner,*
> *Quand rien enfant de Germain observera.*

> Beasts wild with hunger will cross rivers,
> The greatest part of the field will be against Hitler.
> In a cage of iron the great one will be taken,
> When no law is observed by the German child
> Century 2. Quatrain 24

Michel de Nostredame, better known by his Latinized name Nostradamus, was born in St. Remy de Provence on December 14th, 1503 and died July 2nd 1566.

During his lifetime he wrote his predictions in a series of books, or centuries containing 100 quatrains or 4 verse poems. However, century 7 only contains 42 quatrains. This is interesting as the number 42 occurs in both the Bible and the predictions of Paracelcus, but more of that later.

In all he wrote 10 centuries, as well as 141 Presages or Portents, and 58 Sixains, or 6 line poems. I do not intend to delve into the life of Nostradamus as this has been noted in many interpretations of his work. However, from the publication of his works in 1555 to the present time it is accepted that Nostradamus was able to foresee and predict many of the major events that have occurred in the world over the last 440 years.

As I mentioned in the introduction, we must understand how difficult it must have been in the 16th century to understand and interpret the visions that were being seen. Up until the mid 19th century, it was impossible for mankind to perceive powered flight and yet here we are at the end of the 20th century sending probes to Uranus and beyond, and guiding bombs from fighter bombers to within 6 inches of their targets. How difficult it must have been then, and how amazing to see things in visions that could not be comprehended and yet to somehow with the help of comparisons and similarities, describe them in such a way that though obscure before the event, they are revealed as correct after the event.

The famous Hitler quatrain at the beginning must therefore be seen in this light. How else would someone describe the invasion by tanks, armoured cars, aircraft and troops of Europe by Hitler. The number and importance of rivers crossed by the German army in the first line is clear, as is the mention of looting and pillaging (wild with hunger). The second line is only too obvious, as all of Europe was against Hitler, excepting Italy.

Does a cage of iron describe a tank, an armoured car or troop carrier taking the Generals and Hitler himself around the battlefields? I think the fourth line, with the implications of the Hitler youth is obvious.

There is one further clue given to us in this quatrain that makes it all fit into place. Hister could well be a misprint from early translations of Nostradamus' work, but I doubt it. Ister is the Latin name for the River Danube, which rises in Germany and then flows through Austria, Hitler's birthplace.

Here Nostradamus gives us the final clue to this amazing quatrain, not only the name of the person, but his birthplace and the country he will eventually rise to power in.

Pour ne vouloir consentir au divorce,
Qui puis apres sera cogneu indigne,
Le Roi des Isles sera chasse par force
Mis a son lieu que de roi n'aura signe.

For not wishing to consent to the divorce
Which afterwards will be seen as unworthy,
The King of the Islands (Isles) will be chased out,
Replaced instead by one who showed no sign of
becoming King.

Century 10. Quatrain 22

Though no dates are given in this quatrain, the clues are in
the words divorce in the first line, and the third line "Le Roi
des Isles". Edward VIII's abdication was not popular in this
country, and most blamed Mrs. Simpson for him being forced
to flee into exile. George VI was not in line for the throne until
forced to accede after Edward's abdication.

L'oeuvre ancienne se parachevera,
Du toict cherra sur le grand mal ruine:
Innocent faict mort on accusera:
Nocent caiche taillis a la bruine.

The ancient one's work having been accomplished
From the roof evil ruin will fall on the great man,
Being dead, the innocent will be accused of the
deed,
The guilty hidden in the misty woods.

Century 6. Quatrain 37

In the many interpretations of Nostradamus' work I have read,
I have never come across one that attempted to explain this
quatrain, yet to me it seems very self evident. It describes
perfectly the events surrounding November 22nd, 1963. A
day that has been described by most commentators as "the
day everyone remembered exactly what they were doing".

I remember I was sitting with my mother watching television when the death of John Fitzgerald Kennedy was announced. My mother cried. Look again at the scenario described in this quatrain. The first line refers to Pope John XXIII who died on June 3rd 1963, shortly after completing his great Encyclical "Pacem in Terris". Lines 2 and 3 refer directly to Lee Harvey Oswald. It has never been proved that Oswald fired the rifle found on the upper floor of the Dallas Book Repository on that day, but Nostradamus has seen the truth. Oswald could not defend himself after his murder by Jack Ruby, but anyone who has followed the fascinating story of John F. Kennedy's last day knows that the bullet that really killed him came from in front of him and to the right. How many have seen the blurred (misty) photograph of the "grassy knoll" and the rifleman pictured hiding within this small wood. Need I explain more.

Aupres des portes & dedans deux cites
Seront deux fleaux & oncques n'apperceu un tel:
Faim, dedans peste, de fer hors gens boutes,
Crier secours au grand Dieu imortel.

Near the harbours and within two cities
There will be two scourges that have never been seen before:
Hunger, plague within, people thrown out by the iron thing,
They will cry to the great God immortal for help.

Century 2. Quatrain 6

This quatrain is Nostradamus' description of the dropping of atom bombs on Hiroshima and Nagasaki in 1945. Both cities are on the sea, the plague referred to is that of radiation. The rest of this quatrain is, I think, quite self evident. It was of course the first time mankind had used atomic weapons, hence the description of the two scourges in line 2.

So far I have looked at Nostradamus' quatrains that have dealt with one specific event. However, Nostradamus often describes two events in parallel, and in this way we can check even further his amazing insight into the future. There are many quatrains about the Gulf War which I will consider in a later chapter, but on March 25th 1991, Archbishop Lefevre, the leader of the Roman Catholic Traditionalists, died in Econe in Switzerland. The history of Archbishop Lefevre is an interesting one. In 1976 Pope Paul VI and the Vatican Council proclaimed that in future the Roman Catholic Mass would not be conducted in Latin, the language used until that year. Certain Traditionalists lead by Archbishop Lefevre disagreed with the edict and were suspended from the Roman Catholic Church in 1976. Under their new leader the Traditionalists moved from the Vatican to Econe in Switzerland, wholeheartedly rejecting the Second Vatican Council's reforms and continuing to celebrate the Mass of Pius V, Pope from 1566 - 1572.

In 1988 the Vatican Council, under John Paul II, excommunicated Archbishop Lefevre and the Traditionalists, and they remained at Econe until Lefevre's death on March 25th 1991. The Traditionalists are also called the Tonsured Ones. This relates to the Tonsure, or circular shaved area on the top of the head, by which the Traditionalists identify themselves. In French this translates as "Razes" or "Shaven Ones". On March 25th 1991, in the same news broadcast that spoke of the death of Archbishop Lefevre, it was announced that a National Service of Remembrance attended by the Queen and other members of the British Royal Family would be held in the Scottish city of Glasgow on May 4th 1991, to commemorate those killed in the Gulf War. As everyone knows, the Gulf War was continually referred to by President George Bush as the "Just War". Bearing this in mind I find that Nostradamus' prediction of Archbishop Lefevre's death is correct in every detail.

Les deuils laissez, supremes alliances,
Raze Grand mort refus fait en a l'entree:
De retour estre bien fait en oubliance,
La mort du Juste a banquet perpatree.

The battles/duels abandoned, the alliance forces supreme
The great tonsured one will die, having been refused entry to the Church,
In return he will end up a forgotten man,
The dead of the Just war by a communion/ mass will be commemorated.

Presage 57

There can be no doubt about the events mentioned in this fascinating quatrain. Line one deals with the end of the Gulf War and its victors, the alliance forces. Lines two and three are self evident. Line four ties up with line one and predicts the announcement made on the day Archbishop Lefevre died.

Two more quatrains deal decisively with momentous events that are still changing the socio-political face of the world, events that only a few years ago would have seemed impossible.

Es peux & temps chair au poisson donra lieu,
La loi commune sera faicte au contraire:
Vieux tiendra fort puis oste du millieu,
Le Panta chiona philon mis fort arriere.

In those places and times where meat gives way to fish,
The law of communism will be placed in opposition,
The old ones will hold on strongly, then are removed from the scene,
Then all things in common among friends put far behind.

Century 4. Quatrain 32

The clues to this amazing quatrain are to be found in lines 2 and 4. In line 2 the words "La loi commune" translate as "the community law", however, in line 4 Nostradamus changes from old French to Greek. The phrase "Panta chiona philon" is the Greek for all things held in common among friends, quite literally communism. The phrase in line 1 where meat gives way to fish is one of Nostradamus' ways of implying good times followed by hunger.

This quatrain dramatically details the events surrounding the last days of communism in what was the USSR. Gorbachev's reforms, so welcomed in the West, had brought about hard times for the Republic. Prices had risen, grain harvests had failed, crops were left rotting in the fields for lack of transportation and in the major cities people were beginning to go hungry, food shops were beginning to run short.

Disaffected with the results of these new reforms the old guard, hard-line communist leaders until then in opposition, mounted a coup which culminated in the arrest and detainment of Gorbachev in his holiday Dacha in the Crimea on August 19th 1991. However, the old guard had misread public opinion and the power of Boris Yeltsin, the coup collapsed, the leaders were arrested and Gorbachev returned to Moscow on the evening of August 20th. Four days later Gorbachev announced that communism was outlawed in the USSR, having lasted 74 years, and by Christmas day of that year the Soviet red flag had been pulled down all over Russia, the USSR was no more, and even Gorbachev, the architect of perestroika and glasnost had been removed from power. In a book I read some years ago discussing the work of Nostradamus it was interesting to note that the author, whilst translating this quatrain in similar vein to myself, saw the collapse of communism in the USSR as "highly improbable to the point of absurdity". This shows just how unwise it is in this last decade of the 20th century to take for granted the institutions, establishments, governments and agreements that have since 1945, shaped the way that we think, live and govern in the West. The world is beginning to change and mankind must change with it or face the consequences.

The break up of the USSR and the final collapse of the iron curtain, with the countries of eastern Europe beginning to embrace democracy has had affects upon world peace that could hardly have been envisaged a few years ago. Once more, in a chillingly accurate quatrain, Nostradamus predicts the huge upheaval now underway in former Yugoslavia.

Laict, sang grenouilles escoudre en Dalmatie,
Conflict donne, peste pres de Balennes,
Cri sera grand par toute Esclavonie,
Lors naistra monstre pres & de-dans Ravenne.

After the milk of well being, the blood of the people will flow in Dalmatia,
The war having started, a plague will appear near to Balennes,
A great cry will be heard throughout Slovenia,
Then a scourge will be born near and in Ravenna.
Century 2. Quatrain 32

Dalmatia is in Eastern Yugoslavia on the Adriatic coast, its two main towns are Split and Dubrovnik, formerly Ragusa, although in Nostradamus' time it also took in most of Bosnia including the city of Sarajevo. Since 1992 our television screens have been filled with the horrors of civil war in this once beautiful, friendly and prosperous part of eastern Europe. In the second line Nostradamus uses a typical Gallicization to identify the town of Ballenstedt, a town in the north of the former German Democratic Republic. The plague that appears is that of Neo Nazism, which led eventually to wholesale attacks on immigrants and refugees in the north east of a now reunited Germany and continues to spread throughout that country.

Line three is self evident in that Slovenia is that part of former Yugoslavia in the north that we now know as Croatia, whilst the final line of this quatrain refers to the Lombardy League, set up at the same time in northern Italy with the express purpose of dividing Italy into North and South. This, together with the political, business and corruption scandals that appeared in 1992 and a rise in fascism in northern Italy have been seen clearly by Nostradamus in this amazing quatrain and give further credence to his enormous insight into events occurring in the last decade of this century.

In the introduction to this book I stated that it was important to establish the credibility of prophecy by establishing the accuracy of full-filled prophecy. I have used the latter prophecies of Nostradamus to show just how accurate this man was, and of course still is. There are many more extremely accurate predictions, some of which I will talk about later, but my main concern in writing this book is to look forward to the future, not backwards at the past. Suffice to say there are many interpretations of Nostradamus' quatrains in local libraries throughout the world for the reader to investigate.

Theophrastus Baumbast Von Hohenheim, known as Paracelsus, was a contemporary of Nostradamus, but not as well known. I will go into the reasons for this later. Paracelsus was born on 10th November 1493 at Einsiedeln in Switzerland and died 24th September 1541 at Salzburg. He was like Nostradamus, a physician. Again, I do not intend to go into the life of Paracelsus, this has already been documented extremely well by others, in particular in the 11th edition of the Encyclopaedia Britannica.

The prophecies of Paracelsus are set out in 32 prognostications. These prognostications are each accompanied by an occult figure or drawing. The prophecies also contain a Preface and an Elucidation or Epilogue.

Rather than specific events concerning times and places, Paracelsus has set forth his prophecies concerning institutions, establishments, countries and monarchies. He does however, say the following about his prophecies in the Strasburg Edition of the Collected Works of Paracelsus, in his Elucidation or Epilogue.

'The symbolic figures as above stated are 32 and will take their complete course in 42 years'. Unfortunately no starting date is given for the beginning of these 42 years, however it is interesting to find the number 42 occurring in Paracelsus' works, as in Nostradamus' 7th Century.

Bearing in mind the nature of the prophecies of Paracelsus, that they concern institutions, establishments and countries amongst others, it is therefore almost impossible to find Paracelsus to be wise after the event. For most people a Prophet has to be seen to have prophesied an event before they are believed. This I believe, is the reason behind his lack of popularity with commentators and the public alike, because in Paracelsus' case, he prophesied the fall of all our major beliefs and institutions and the coming of God. In the Elucidation of the Prognostication he says concerning the prophecies;

> *'He does not indeed each year do away with one symbol, but simultaneously fulfils them all and altogether as one, until all is completed and accomplished'.*

What he is saying here is that even though he has said they will take their complete course in 42 years, all the institutions, monarchies and establishments will fall together, slowly at first, and then moving inexorably towards their complete collapse over a period of 42 years. Amongst the 32 prognostications are at least 2 that forecast the end of the Roman Catholic Church.

These very specific prognostications will be discussed in detail in the chapter "The Vatican and the Papacy" and correspond with much that Nostradamus has to say concerning the Roman Catholic Church. However, included in the prognostications is the one very specifically phrased elucidation to a time of very great change and at the end of the prognostication, a date is given. This date is the same date given by both Nostradamus and the Bible for the day of Judgement, or as it is described in the Koran, the day of Resurrection.

Saint Malachy is one of the lesser known prophets, certainly not as well known as Nostradamus, but nevertheless the prophecies of Malachy are in many ways, even more astounding than those of other more illustrious prophets.

Saint Malachy was born in Armagh, Ireland in 1094, some 900 years ago. In 1132 he became Primate of Armagh and his death occurred in 1148 at Clairvaux, where he died in the arms of his friend and colleague Saint Bernard of Clairvaux. In 1139 Malachy visited Rome and it is thought that during this visit he received his visions and having committed them to paper, gave them to Pope Innocent II. What those visions contained were the names of every Pope, starting in 1143 with Celestine II and continuing through one hundred and eleven Popes, until he reaches the last Pope of the Roman Catholic Church.

Saint Malachy gives each Pope in his list a phrase or sentence in Latin that in some way describes that particular Pope. Sometimes the phrase, or epithet as they have been called, describes the Popes' armorial bearings on his coat of arms, hence Pope Leo XIII, who was elected by the Conclave in 1878 had as Malachy's epithet "Lumen in Caelo", translated as light in the sky. Indeed his coat of arms featured a blazing comet in the heavens.

At other times however, Malachy alludes to the Popes' background and his influence within the Roman Catholic Church. The epithet of Pope John XXIII describes in perfect detail these two things. Pope John XXIII was one of the most loved of all Popes and was a true pastor to his flock, his Papacy culminating in his Encyclical "Pacem in Terris", considered to be one of the most impressive and important documents of all time. It was published in the year of his death, 1963, and is alluded to by Nostradamus in Century 6, Quatrain 37.

"L'oeuvre ancienne se parachevera" translating as "the work of the ancient one having been accomplished". The rest of the quatrain deals with the killing of John F Kennedy, in November 1963 shortly after the publication of "Pacem in Terris" and the death of John XXIII. Before becoming Pope in 1958, he was appointed Patriach of Venice in 1953, where he travelled to and fro through the canals of that great city in his gondola, attending to the needs of the flock of the Sea of Venice. His epithet Pastor et Nauta, translated as Pastor and Mariner describes his Papacy in perfect detail.

In the long list of 112 Popes given by Malachy, we have now reached number 110, John Paul II, whose motto *"De Labore Solis"* translates as "the work of the sun". If one accepts that quite literally the sun goes around the earth spreading its light, then John Paul II's epithet is once again perfect. Pope John Paul II's reign has been one of the most media documented of all Popes, with the most prominent image of his Papacy being that of him kissing the ground during his journeys as the most travelled Pope ever, spreading the light of Christianity to every corner of the earth. However, if this explanation sounds a little far fetched, there is another far more plausible explanation for John Paul II's epithet "the work of the sun".

In 1979 John Paul II commissioned a Papal enquiry into the Roman Catholic Church's attitude towards Galileo. Galileo, born in 1564 was the Italian scientist, mathematician and astronomer who proclaimed against the teachings of the Catholic Church, that the world was not the centre of the universe and that as Copernicus had stated the earth rotated around the sun and not the sun around the earth. Indeed in 1616 the Roman Catholic Church announced the Edict of Inquisition against Galileo's astronomical pronouncements. On the 30th October 1992, after the Papal commission had spent 13 years considering "the work of the sun", John Paul II announced that Galileo had been forgiven and that indeed, the earth rotated around the sun. Surely the epithet of John Paul II is now no longer in doubt. Nostradamus has his own epithet for John Paul II and it is based very much on Malachy's prophecy. In Century 8, quatrain 46 he describes John Paul II as:-

"Pol mensolee....."
and in Century 5, quatrain 29 as:-
"Pol Mansol....."

Here, Nostradamus alludes to Malachy's epithet of the "work of the sun" by using a typical Nostradamus trick of combining French with Latin, using a combination of the Latin word 'manus' man's work or labour, with the French 'soleil' or sun. A further allusion is made by Nostradamus not only to the Pope's Christian name Paul, but also his birthplace Poland, hence, "Pol Mansol".

In the chapter "The Vatican and the Papacy" this will be discussed in more depth. Suffice to say that there are two more Popes to come after John Paul II according to Malachy and the last Pope, Petrus Romanus or Peter the Roman has after his name this chilling prophecy.

In the final persecution of the Holy Roman Empire there will reign Peter the Roman, who will feed his flock among many tribulations, after which the seven hilled city will be destroyed and the dreadful Judge will judge the people.

If Saint Malachy is not too well known, Saint Columbkille or Saint Columba as he is often known, is, outside of Ireland, even more obscure, but nevertheless just as important. His predictions are part of Irish folklore and his life is well documented. Born in County Donegal in 521 AD, he attended monastic school in Moville, before entering the monastery of Clonard. In 563 AD he left Ireland for Iona, where he spent the remaining 32 years of his life as Abbot of Iona.

His prophecies are contained in letters he wrote in poetic form to his friend Saint Brendan. The poems refer to a time he calls "the latter ages"

There shall come times of dark affliction
Of scarcity, of sorrow, and of wailing;
In the latter ages of the world's existence
The Prophecies of St Columbkille verse 6

In the letter entitled "Saint Columbkille Cecinit" he alludes to a promise made to Saint Patrick by God after he had expelled all the demons from Ireland.

I concede as a favour to them without deception,
and Saint Patrick did concede the same;
That seven years before the last day,
The sea shall submerge Eire by one inundation.
Saint Columbkille Cecinit verse 64

Though this event may seem highly unlikely I will show in later chapters how all the prophets forecast major natural disasters, including flooding, storms, earthquakes and volcanic eruptions occurring as we move through the latter days.

Chapter 2
Judgement Day

But of that day and hour knoweth no man, no, not
the angels of heaven, but my father only.

Matthew 24. verse 36

For hundreds of years mankind has been predicting the end of the world, the second coming, the resurrection, the final judgement. Hardly a decade goes by without at least one group of people announcing the date of the Apocalypse. How these dates are arrived at varies, but very few if any are based upon the predictions and indeed dates that are given in the Bible, Nostradamus and Paracelsus. Not only do the Bible, Nostradamus and Paracelsus give the same date for this "great change" but as if to confirm that this date is correct, the Bible also gives the three most important dates in the history of the Jewish people since the destruction of the second temple in 70 AD.

For over a thousand years the interpretations of these dates have been incorrect, due to two inherent errors made almost two thousand years ago. Indeed, the key to this mystery goes back almost to the seventh century BC, a key which when used to interpret both the Old and New Testament prophecies, reveals the Bible's greatest secrets.

$$E4 \ (5 + 6) + D8 \ (6+14) = 1967 \ ©$$

I invented the preceding equation in order to give very simply and specifically, the key to the Bible's mysterious datings. The equation is both mathematical, historical and biblical and will become clear to the reader as the chapter unfolds.

First however, two mistakes in biblical interpretation have to be identified and rectified before we progress. The first mistake concerns an event that ranks as one of the most important in the history not only of the Jewish faith, but of

Christians and Muslims alike. It is the "abomination of the desolation".

> *And arms shall stand on his part, and they shall pollute the sanctuary of strength, and shall take away the daily sacrifice, and they shall place the abomination that maketh desolate.*
>
> Daniel 11. verse 31

In "A Dictionary of the Bible" published at the beginning of this century, James Hastings MA DD analyses the different interpretations of the above verse and concludes that it refers to "The setting up by Antiochus Epiphanes of a small idol/altar on the altar of the Holy Temple in Jerusalem in 167 BC".

This refers to the invasion and capture of Jerusalem by the Seleucids under Antiochus in 167 BC, an event that spawned the Maccabean revolution, which after the death of Judas Maccabeus in battle in 160 BC was successful in expelling the Seleucids from Jerusalem.

To this very day theologians and scholars alike have accepted this interpretation of the "abomination that maketh desolate". However, they are wrong. Daniel the sixth century prophet, is not the only place in the Bible where this event is mentioned. It is also mentioned emphatically in two of the New Testament gospels and is spoken about by Jesus Christ himself.

> *When ye therefore shall see the abomination of desolation, spoken of by Daniel the prophet, stand in the holy place, (whoso readeth let him understand).*
>
> St Matthew 24. verse 15

> *But when ye shall see the abomination of desolation, spoken of by Daniel the prophet, standing where it ought not, (let him that readeth understand).*
>
> St Mark 13. verse 14

These two verses allude to the conversation between Jesus, Peter, James, John and Andrew on the Mount of Olives shortly after Jesus has admonished the Pharisees and Sadducees in the temple, just two days before the feast of the Passover. Before he mentions the "abomination" Jesus says the following to his disciples admiring the grandeur of the temple.

> *Seest thou these great buildings? there shall not be left one stone upon another, that shall not be thrown down.*
>
> St Mark 13. verse 2

Here Jesus is prophesying an event that is to take place within the lifetime of the disciples. In 70 AD the Roman Legions under Titus Andronichus, son of Emperor Titus Flavius Vespasian, on the orders of Nero before his death captured and destroyed Jerusalem, in doing so completely razing the Temple of the Jews to the ground.

As Jesus places the event of the "abomination" after the destruction of the temple in 70 AD and also uses the words "when ye shall see" (Mark 13 verse 14), therefore placing this event in the future tense, it is impossible that the "abomination that maketh desolate" took place in 167 BC. However, there are many clues that point to the correct date, the first of these being in the preceding gospel verses.

The inclusion of the words in brackets in Matthew 24 verse 15 and Mark 13 verse 14 are a clear indication that the reader should pay very great attention to the verse and in particular the sentence immediately before the brackets. Therefore the words "stand in the holy place" (who so readeth let him understand) and "standing where it ought not" (let him that readeth understand) must be considered as the most important part of these verses.

What both verses are saying is that the "abomination" will be placed somewhere that is not only a "holy place", but also a place or position that under normal circumstances would be forbidden to it. Within the Jewish faith the words "holy place" in biblical terms means only one thing, the Holy Temple in Jerusalem.

After its destruction in 70 AD the Holy Temple was never rebuilt. The ground on which the Temple had stood, the Temple Mount, remained beyond the Western or Wailing wall as the holiest place of Judaism. However, it was not to remain so. In 638 AD, six years after the death of Mohammed, Abu Bakr the first caliph of Islam, invaded and captured Jerusalem. On the death of Abu Bakr, Omar ibn al Khattab, advisor to Mohammed became the second caliph. It was on Omar's orders that a magnificent golden domed mosque was built on the site of the old Temple. The construction of Islam's third holiest shrine, standing directly over the holiest place of the Jews on the temple mount began in 688 AD. The Mosque of Omar ibn al Khattab, the Dome of the Rock. This is the true identification of the "abomination that maketh desolate".

From 688 AD the Jewish people were not only without a homeland but they had been denied access to their holiest place of worship. As a people and a nation they were indeed desolate.

Having identified and rectified the first interpretative error in the Bible, it is time to search for the second. This time we are not looking for a starting date by which to measure our timings, but at the timings themselves.

> *But the court which is without the temple leave out, and measure it not; for it is given unto the Gentiles: and the holy city shall they tread under foot forty and two months.*
> *And I will give power unto my two witnesses, and they shall prophesy a thousand two hundred and three score days, clothed in sackcloth.*
> Revelation 11. verses 2 & 3

The first thing that seems clear in these two verses is that they appear to be talking about the same time scale. If an average month is thirty days, then the forty two months of verse 2 coincides exactly with the one thousand two hundred and sixty days of verse 3.

However, if we take reckonings from the Julian calendar which calculated a year as measuring three hundred and sixty five and a quarter days, then taking into account the extra day for a leap year, the period of forty two months would be equal to one thousand two hundred and seventy nine days.

The other two facts we know from these verses is that in verse 1 the area outside the temple will be in the hands of the Gentiles, i.e. non Jewish people as will the holy city of Jerusalem for that amount of time; and in verse 2 the two witnesses of God, in other words the Houses of Judah and Israel, the Jewish people will prophesy or preach for a similar period "clothed in sackcloth". Sackcloth is symbolic of regret and repentance and the ancient custom of wearing sackcloth signified penitence and mourning.

What these two verses are saying is that the Jewish people will lose their place of worship including the city of Jerusalem; it will be given over to non Jewish people for a specific period of time. This coincides with a similar period of time during which the Jewish people are in mourning not only for the loss of their place of worship, but of their homeland.

And she brought forth a man child, who was to rule all nations with a rod of iron: and her child was caught up unto God, and to his throne.
And the woman fled into the wilderness, where she hath a place prepared of God, that they should feed her a thousand two hundred and threescore days.

Revelation 12. verses 5 & 6

Once again one thousand two hundred and sixty days are mentioned here and refer to a time spent in the wilderness. The woman referred to, who is to bring forth a manchild who will rule all nations with a rod of iron is not only symbolic of Mary the mother of Jesus, but of the entire Jewish nation. Once again these two verses prophesy that the Jewish nation will wander in the wilderness for one thousand two hundred and sixty days.

In every interpretation of the Bible I have read, this period of time, both one thousand two hundred and sixty days and forty two months, are described as approximating the three and a half years between the setting up of the idol/altar by Antiochus in 167 BC and the recapturing of the Holy Temple by Judas Maccabeus and his followers in 163 BC. The latter date however, is a spurious one that has not been conclusively proven. Even after the death of Maccabeus in 160 BC the struggle between the Jews and the Seleucids continued. The other notable problem with this interpretation is that it concerns events before the birth of Christ. Revelation, as I have stated in chapter one was written by Saint John on Patmos around 70 AD. At that time the whole of the middle east was aware of such historical facts, so why make prophecies about events already passed. This does not make sense. And why bother giving a specific timing if it is only approximately correct. There can only be one answer and that is that previous interpretations of these timings are in error.

The correct interpretations of these timings is however, very specific and can only be arrived at by finding the key to these extraordinary prophecies. A key that when turned gives us the most incredible set of dates.

For I have laid upon thee the years of their iniquity, according to the number of the days, three hundred and ninety days: so shalt thou bear the iniquity of the house of Israel.

And when thou hast accomplished them, lie again
on thy right side, and thou shalt bear the iniquity
of the house of Judah forty days: I have
appointed thee each day for a year.

Ezekiel 4. verses 5 & 6

In these two consecutive verses from the Old Testament book of Ezekiel, we are given the key to unlocking the Bible's greatest secrets. Ezekiel was given these instructions in the year 581 BC.

In the fifth day of the month, which was the fifth
year of King Jehoiachin's captivity.

Ezekiel 1. verse 2

Jehoiachin was taken captive to Babylon by Nebuchadnezzar after the capture of Jerusalem in 586 BC. The instruction that each day should count as a year, though given to Ezekiel specifically, would have been understood by the other biblical prophets as applying to them also. Daniel, a keen scholar and student of Ezekiel would have seen this instruction as applying to himself. Writing some thirty years after Ezekiel the words "I have appointed thee each day for a year" were to Daniel, the true word of God and as such became constant.

Therefore the three hundred and ninety "days" refers to the three hundred and ninety years from the House of Israel's capture and deportation to Nineveh in 722 BC to their return to Jerusalem after Alexader's conquest in 332BC. The forty "days" refers to the forty years of the House of Judah's deportation to Babylon after the capture of Jerusalem by Nebuchadnezza.

Having now identified and rectified the second error in biblical interpretations, we can apply them to the timings given in the Bible with incredible results. Saint John, writing the Revelation would also have been aware of the instruction that each day should be counted as a year and so the "one thousand two hundred and threescore days" of Revelation chapters 11 and 12, become years. Taking the dates of the "abomination that maketh desolate" as the beginning of the period of Jewish desolation, we have 688 AD. If one adds one thousand two hundred and sixty "years" to this date we arrive at the year 1948. On May 14th 1948 the British mandate for Palestine ended and the State of Israel was created. For the first time since 688 AD the Jewish faith once again had a homeland.

Though this was indeed a historic date for the Jewish people there was a problem. The new state of Israel only incorporated West Jerusalem. East Jerusalem, including the Temple Mount and the Dome of the Rock were in Jordanian territory and as such Palestinian and therefore a mixture of Christianity and Islam. The boundary between East or Old Jerusalem and West Jerusalem most predominately signified by the West or Wailing Wall. From May 14th 1948 the Jewish people may have had a homeland, but at that time they did not control their holiest of holies, the Temple Mount. This situation was however, to change.

> *And he said unto me, Unto two thousand and three hundred days, then shall the sanctuary be cleansed.*
>
> Daniel 8. verse 14

To understand fully the importance of this verse we must first study the previous verse to find exactly what the two thousand three hundred days refer to.

> *How long shall be the vision concerning the daily sacrifice, and the transgression of desolation, to give both the sanctuary and the host to be trampled under foot.*
>
> Daniel 8. verse 13

Here Daniel is told that the two thousand three hundred days mark the time that Jerusalem, the sanctuary and the host, the

Temple Mount, will be under the domination of the Gentiles. Daniel is also told that the starting date for this period is the beginning of his vision. The vision that Daniel is given in chapter 8 is most specific and starts with one of the greatest events of pre Christian history.

Then I lifted up mine eyes, and saw, and, behold, there stood before the river a ram which had two horns: and the two horns were high; but one was higher than the other, and the higher came up last.
Daniel 8. verse 3

Further on in the same chapter Daniel is given an explanation of this verse.

The ram which thou savest having two horns are the Kings of Media and Persia.
Daniel 8. verse 20

The first Persian King to also be King of the Medes was Darius I (548 - 486 BC). The last of the Persian Kings was Darius III, defeated in one of the most significant battles in history.

Further information as to a starting date for the vision is then given.

And as I was considering, behold, an he goat came from the west on the face of the whole earth, and touched not the ground: and the he goat had a notable horn between his eyes.
Daniel 8. verse 5

Once again a further explanation is given.

And the rough goat is the King of Grecia; and that great horn that is between his eyes is the first King.
Daniel 8. verse 21

The clues to these verses are in the words "and touched not the ground" and the single word "great".

We have identified the ram as being the Persian Empire, the goat signifies the Greek Empire led by Alexander the Great, the first commander to lead his army on horseback, his feet not touching the ground.

And he came to that ram that had two horns, which I had seen standing before the river, and ran into him in his fury and his power.

Daniel 8. verse 6

What Daniel is seeing in his vision is a battle, between the Persian Empire and the Greeks led by Alexander which takes place across a river. There is only one battle this could possibly be. It is the Battle of Issus, which took place across the River Penaris on what is now the Mediterranean coast of south east Turkey, just north of Syria. In the battle Alexander defeated the Persian army and their leader King Darius III. The date of this battle was 333 BC. Taking this as the starting date of the vision and considering Ezekiel's instruction to count every day as a year, adding two thousand three hundred years to 333 BC gives us the year 1967. On June 5th 1967 Israel launched a lightning attack on its neighbours at the beginning of the Six Day War. In the first few minutes of the war the Israeli army surrounded and sealed off East Jerusalem and claimed it as Israeli territory. For the first time since the capture of Jerusalem and destruction of the temple by Titus in 70 AD the people of Israel not only had their own state but once again controlled their holiest of holies, the Temple Mount.

This then is the key to the Bible's greatest mystery. Verses five and six of chapter 4 of Ezekiel, taken together with verses six and fourteen of Daniel chapter 8 give the year 1967. Hence the equation;

$$E4(5+6) + D8(6+14) = 1967. ©$$

As if to clarify this date even more conclusively, verse two of Revelation chapter 11, if calculated by the Julian calendar corresponds exactly.

> *And the holy city shall they tread under foot forty and two months.*
>
> Revelation 11. verse 2

As I said earlier in the chapter, this corresponds in the Julian calendar to one thousand two hundred and seventy nine days. If you convert this to years and add it to the date 688 AD we once again arrive at the year 1967.

There are two further dates that are given in the Book of Daniel and these must be looked at applying the same rules.

> *And from the time that the daily sacrifice shall be taken away, and the abomination that maketh desolate set up, there shall be a thousand two hundred and ninety days.*
>
> Daniel 12. verse 11

In the first part of this verse we are given the starting date of 688 AD, the date that the "abomination that maketh desolate" was set up. If you add to this date one thousand two hundred and ninety "years" instead of days we arrive at the year 1978. On September 17th 1978 after months of negotiation, one of the most extraordinary events of this century took place. President Jimmy Carter of the USA, Egyptian President Anwar Sadat and Israel's Prime Minister Menachem Begin signed the Camp David Agreement. For the first time since the Exodus from Egypt in 1290 BC, Israel was at peace with its Arab neighbour.

So now the Bible has correctly given us the three most important dates in the history of the Jewish people this century; 1948, 1967 and 1978. There is however, one more date given within the pages of Daniel, a date yet to come, a date of enormous significance.

Blessed is he that waiteth and cometh to the thousand three hundred and five and thirty days.
Daniel 12. verse 12

The interesting word in this verse is "Blessed". Although used often in the Bible, it is a word which is always descriptive of a state of grace that each individual can attain, a oneness with God, a state of redemption. It can perhaps be better understood in this verse from Revelation.

Blessed is he that hath part in the first resurrection.
Revelation 20. verse 6

In this verse the "first resurrection" refers to an apocalyptic event in our future, an event described in the preceding verse of Revelation.

And I saw thrones, and they that sat upon them, and judgement was given unto them: and I saw the souls of them that were beheaded for the witness of Jesus, and for the word of God, and which had not worshipped the beast, neither his image, neither had received his mark upon their foreheads, or in their hands; and they lived and reigned with Christ a thousand years.
But the rest of the dead lived not again until the thousand years were finished. This is the first resurrection.
Revelation 20. verses 4 & 5

These two verses reveal the enormity of the message given in the last verse of the Book of Daniel. Within the verse he is telling us that those who reach the "one thousand three hundred and five and thirty days", being blessed, have passed beyond Judgement Day, or as it is described in the Koran, "the day of resurrection". Once again we must obey the instruction laid down by Ezekiel and count those days as years and again the starting point for our calculations is the "abomination that maketh desolate", in other words 688 AD. Adding one thousand three hundred and thirty five years to this date gives us the year 2023. Having been given this final dating Daniel is then told, in the last verse of his book:-

But go thy way till the end be: for thou shalt rest, and stand in thy lot at the end of the days.
Daniel 12. verse 13

The finality of this last verse is unequivocal and relates directly to the penultimate verse stating as it does that those who reach the "one thousand three hundred and five and thirty days" are not only "blessed" but will have reached the "end of the days". That the Bible is correct in its first three datings of 1948, 1967 and 1978 cannot be in doubt. Who then can doubt that the final dating given is not also correct. It is a date that immediately follows Armageddon: Judgement Day, the day of Resurrection. A cataclysmic event that will change the world. The date is 2023.

It is not only the Bible that gives us the date 2023. Both Nostradamus and Paracelsus give the same date and the time-scale of Saint Malachy's prophecies fits exactly. Using simple arithmetic and two quatrains of Nostradamus we arrive not only at the correct date but are given a frightening scenario of the future to come.

Chef d'Aries, Jupiter & Saturne,
Dieu eternel quelles mutations?
Puis par long siecle son maling temps retourne
Gaule, & Italie quelles emotions?
Jupiter and Saturn joined in Aries,
Eternal God what changes.
When after a long century the bad times will return
In France and Italy what turmoil.
Century 1. Quatrain 51

The conjunction of Jupiter and Saturn in Aries is very rare last occurring almost two hundred years ago. The next time this astronomical conjunction occurred was the 2nd September 1995. The third line brings this quatrain into the present time, as Nostradamus refers to the 20th century as the long century. The changes and turmoil in Italy and France are already underway, with political scandals and uncertainty in Italy and the problems in France between the establishment and the perceived threat from Islamic extremism. It seems that Nostradamus sees the 2nd September 1995 as the starting point for a major catastrophe.

> *Celeste feu du coste d'Occident,*
> *Et du midy, courir jusqu'au Levant,*
> *Vers demy morts sans poinct trouver racine*
> *Troisieme aage, a Mars le belliqueux,*
> *Des Escarboucles on verra briller feux,*
> *Aage Escarboucle, et a la fin famine.*

Fire from the heavens will strike the West,
And the Muslim world will rush upon Israel,
People will die of hunger without finding a root to feed on
This is the third world war, the fury of the Gods of war,
The revolutionaries will light their flaming fires,
The war of revolution, and at the finish will be famine.

Sixain 27

Nostradamus uses the word "midy" or people of the south, to denote the world of Islam. Some people have claimed the word "Levant" as applying to the Isle de Levant, a small island off the coast of France close to Hyeres. Others have claimed it signifies Japan, as in "soleil levant" or the "rising sun". However, in Nostradamus' time it would have been understood as the Levant Coast, stretching from Syria through Lebanon and Israel to the Egyptian border in the eastern Mediterranean. The word "Escarboucle" means carbuncle or garnet which is poppy or blood red and signifies revolution. The famine mentioned at the end of the sixain is of world wide proportions.

It appears then that Nostradamus sees the beginnings of this calamity as having started on the 2nd September 1995. We now have to find the duration of these troubles.

> *L'antechrist trois bien tost annichilez,*
> *Vignt & sept ans sang durera sa guerre.*
> *Les heretiques mortz, captifs, exilez.*
> *Sang corps humain eau rougi gresler terre.*

The third antichrist is soon annihilated,
His bloody war will have lasted twenty seven years.
The heretics/unbelievers are dead, captured, exiled.
The blood of human bodies will redden the whole earth.

Century 8. Quatrain 77

Nostradamus mentions three antichrists in his quatrains. The first is Napoleon, the second Hitler and the third the "man from the east".

> *Tant attendu ne reviendra jamais*
> *Dedans l'Europe, en Asie apparoistra*
> *Un de la ligue islu du grand Hermes,*
> *Et sur tous rois des orientz croistra.*

Long awaited he will never return in Europe,
in Asia he will appear
One of the league issued from the great Hermes,
and he will have power above all the kings of the East.

Century 10. Quatrain 75

In Hermetic terms the God Hermes stands for Mercury and Jupiter indicating Islam. I will deal in more depth with the

Antichrist in a later chapter, suffice to say that Jean Dixon, the well known American prophetess also talks about the Antichrist as the "man from the East" claiming he was born in 1962 and, as the antithesis of Jesus Christ, he will appear on the world stage aged 33 in 1995.

Nostradamus therefore states that the problems the Antichrist starts will last for twenty seven years. If we take the starting date as 2nd September 1995, these problems come to an end sometime after 2nd September 2022. On the very doorstep of the Bible's dating of 2023.

Exactly the same date is given by Paracelsus in the Twenty Ninth Figure of his prognostications. The figure shows a lamb with a bishop's mitre on its head feeding beneath a tree, accompanied by the following prognostication.

> *'Thus shall it come to pass that each one will be led into its own pasture. For feeding in strange pasture causeth distress, contention, and misery in this world. As soon as each one cometh into its own stall there shall be unity. For the mouth becometh depraved, feeding according to its lust as it pleaseth the jaws; all that cometh of going into strange pastures. How blessed shall be the hour, and the poverty, that will come and shall ordain each one to its meadow, not far from the year XXXXIII.'*
>
> Paracelsus. Figure 29

As mentioned in the first chapter, most of the prognostications of Paracelsus concern countries, institutions, establishments and monarchies. Figure twenty nine however seems to refer to the individual and in particular to a state of change that each individual can reach. This corresponds to the great change that is forecast in the Bible, a total renewal, a resurrection. The date given at the end of the prognostication is however confusing. In Roman numerology there is no such number. At first it appears the number could be forty three, but in Roman numerals this would be XLIII, in other words fifty minus ten plus three. The fact that Paracelsus tells us this is a year is the clue to the correct interpretation of the figure. Indeed, looked at in this light there is only one date it can possibly be and that is 2023. The words "not far from the year" seem to indicate, as does Nostradamus, that this great change will have occurred by the year 2023. As stated earlier the Bible says that those who reach 2023 are "blessed". So it would seem that by the year 2023 we will have passed through Armageddon and Judgement Day and arrived at a state of total renewal.

Paracelsus gives two more datings in his prophecies, firstly in his Preface to the Prognostications and then in his Elucidations of the Prognostications and if these are compared with the Nostradamus quatrain that gives the dating of the beginning of this catastrophe, we once again reach the year 2023.

> *"To describe the courses this world will pass through in 24 years is lamentable enough. That man should have made himself so greedy and should have so wholly deluded himself and have failed to realise that his days must needs thereby be shortened".*
>
> Preface to the Prognostications of Paracelsus

The first sentence appears to describe a period of conflict, calamity and warfare lasting for twenty four years. This period of twenty four years is also mentioned in the Elucidations.

> *"This one has often brought about peace, and has thereafter brought peace to himself. But he has many times been again awakened. When he rouses himself all creatures tremble before him. He is that that reverses and judges as seems good to him, and he has determined to act yet 24 years*

until again he rests. To him such time is but a moment. To us he leaves the tedious length thereof".
Elucidations to the Prognostications of Paracelsus

The first part of this Elucidation appears to be a specific reference to a power that is able to not only judge mankind, but to change times. The fact that "all creatures tremble before him" further strengthens the description. The awakening of this power is similar to Daniel's prophecy of the final conflict.

"And at that time shall Michael stand up, the great prince which standeth for the children of thy people; and there shall be a time of trouble, such as never was since there was a nation even to that same time: and at that time thy people shall be delivered, every one that shall be found written in the book".
Daniel 12. verse 1

It would appear that what Paracelsus is saying in both the Preface and the Elucidation concerns a world wide tribulation lasting twenty four years that ends with Judgement Day. The last sentence of the Preface indicates that because of mans greed and delusion his "days must needs thereby be shortened". This corresponds to a similar reference in the Elucidations to the Prognostications and also to a remark made by Jesus to his disciples on the Mount of Olives.

"Although God has for a long time looked on to see what man would do, and how he would apply his wisdom, yet it is directed to nothing permanent nor certain, albeit he so persuades himself. This must cease".
Elucidations of the Prognostications of Paracelsus

"And except those days should be shortened there should no flesh be saved: but for the elect's sake those days shall be shortened".
St. Matthew 24. verse 22

The scenario that appears from Paracelsus is one of major catastrophe and tribulation, culminating in Armageddon, God's intervention and Judgement Day. The tribulations will last twenty four years and it appears Nostadamus has given us the starting date.

L'an mil neuf cens nonante neuf sept mois,
Du ciel viendra un grand Roi deffraieur.
Resusciter le grand Roi d'Angolmois.
Avant que Mars regner par bon heur.

In the year 1999 seven months,
From the sky will come a great King of terror.
Bringing back to life the great King of the Mongols.
Before and after war reigns happily.
Century 10. Quatrain 72

This is one of the most famous of all the Nostradamus quatrains. I discuss the interpretation of this ambiguous prophecy in the penultimate chapter of the book, but if we take this date literally as the start of the tribulations, and Paracelsus tells us they will last 24 years, once again we arrive at the year 2023.

There is one more prophecy which though not being numerically specific, corresponds to the same time scale mentioned in the previous pages. The dating is given in parable form by Jesus Christ during his conversation with the Apostles on the Mount of Olives two days before the Passover. The Apostles ask Jesus,

When shall these things be? and what shall be the sign of thy coming, and of the end of the world.
Saint Matthew 24. verse 3

Jesus then speaks of the great tribulations that shall befall mankind before the great judgement.

> And then shall appear the sign of the Son of man in heaven; and then shall all the tribes of the earth mourn, and they shall see the Son of man coming in the clouds of heaven with power and great glory.
> Saint Matthew 24. verse 30

Jesus follows this with a parable that gives a quite specific time period for the events he has spoken of earlier.

> Now learn a parable of the fig tree; when his branch is yet tender and putteth forth leaves, ye know that summer is nigh:
> So likewise ye, when ye shall see all these things, know that it is near, even at the doors.
> Saint Matthew 24. verses 32-33

In Biblical terms the fig tree is always symbolic of Israel. As we have seen earlier in the chapter the State of Israel came into being on May 14th 1948. What this verse is alluding to is a young State of Israel, its population spreading across the country and becoming fruitful. Since 1967 and the six day war, this is indeed what Israel has done, moving as it has into the West Bank, Gaza Strip, Sinai and the Golan Heights and creating new settlements, turning arid desert into fertile land. The warning given in verse thirty three is very specific, saying as it does that when the world sees Israel growing as a nation, then the tribulations he has forecast will come about. The next two verses are even more specific and give a time scale for these events that coincides with the other prophetic timings perfectly.

> Verily I say unto you, this generation shall not pass, till all these things be fulfilled.
> Heaven and earth shall pass away, but my words shall not pass away.
> Saint Matthew 24. verses 34-35

What Jesus is saying here is simply that the generation that sees the State of Israel come into being, and start to expand will be the generation that witnesses the terrible tribulations he has spoken about and will also be witnesses to the "coming of the Son of man". Those people therefore, born between 1947 and 1967 are the generation that will witness the most tremendous upheaval mankind has experienced since the great flood. A time of natural disasters, revolution, famine and war on an unprecedented scale and at the finish - Judgement Day.

The message Jesus gives us in chapter 24 of Saint Matthew's gospel tells us who will witness this event . It is an event that will be seen by that generation of mankind that has seen the formation of the State of Israel. We are that generation.

Chapter 3
The Beast

*Here is wisdom. Let him that hath understanding
count the number of the beast: for it is the number
of a man; and his number is six hundred three
score and six.*
Revelation 13. verse 18

This is perhaps, one of the most misunderstood and
misinterpreted verses in the Bible. Most scholars and
commentators have attributed the Beast and the number 666
as representing one individual, the Antichrist. Indeed, there
have been many films over the last twenty years depicting
this idea. However to do this is to oversimplify and
misunderstand the true meaning. The final verse of
Revelation chapter 13 has to be taken in context with the
preceding seventeen verses in order to gain a clear picture of
the beast and its true identity.

*And I stood upon the sand of the sea, and saw a
beast rise up out of the sea, having seven heads
and ten horns, and upon his horns ten crowns, and
upon his heads the name of blasphemy.*
Revelation 13. verse 1

In the first part of this verse John sees the beast rising up out
of the sea, and from this description it appears John is
indicating that the beast is a land rising up out of the sea, but
what of the seven heads and the ten horns. In Revelation
chapter 17 John once again sees the beast in a vision.

*So he carried me away in the spirit into the
wilderness: and I saw a woman sit upon a scarlet
coloured beast, full of names of blasphemy, having
seven heads and ten horns.*
Revelation 17. verse 3

John himself marvels at this vision, and is then given the translation of the vision further on in the same chapter.

> *And here is the mind which hath wisdom. The seven heads are seven mountains, on which the woman sitteth.*
>
> Revelation 17. verse 9

> *And the ten horns which thou sawest are ten kings, which have received no Kingdom as yet; but receive power as Kings one hour with the beast.*
>
> Revelation 17. verse 12

What John has seen is a land with at its centre, seven mountains, and within this land ten kings or kingdoms that are in league with the beast, or the land. A further description follows:

> *And the beast which I saw was like unto a leopard, and his feet were as the feet of a bear, and his mouth as the mouth of a lion: and the dragon gave him his power, and his seat, and great authority.*
>
> Revelation 13. verse 2

Here John, in an incredibly succinct and graphic way, is showing us the form and nature of this land he sees rising from the sea, and even uses terminology which brings the description into the 20th Century. The final clue to this appears in the next verse.

> *And I saw one of his heads as it were wounded to death, and his deadly wound was healed: and all the world wondered after the beast.*
>
> Revelation 13. verse 3

Here, John brings his description of the beast firmly into the latter half of the 20th Century. In verse 2 of Revelation 13, John is describing the land of Greater Europe. The leopard has always been the beast associated with greater Germany, and here John tells us that the beast, this great land is like a leopard, but has the feet of a bear. The bear has always been Russia, and if one takes a map of greater Europe it can be seen that the body of Europe, the leopard is greater Germany, the feet Russia, and looking to the head of the beast, John describes its mouth as the mouth of a lion. The lion is of course, the symbol of Britain. It is almost as if John has seen a map of greater Europe, and has then described the parameters of this huge land mass in 20th Century terms. More clues emerge with the description of the seven heads. John is told these seven heads are seven mountains upon which a woman sits, but who or what is this woman. The answer is given in Revelation Chapter 17.

And the woman which thou sawest is that great city, which reigneth over the kings of the earth.
Revelation 17. verse 18

So we now know that this great beast, has at its centre a city that sits on seven mountains. There is only one city in the world that this can be, and as every school child is told, Rome the Eternal City, is built on seven hills.

We have now not only identified the beast as being greater Europe, but have also established Rome as its head, its centre, its power base. So what of the ten horns on the beast. We are told in Revelation 17 verse 12 that these ten horns are ten kings, and these ten kings will receive "power as kings one hour with the beast". What John is describing here is a confederacy of ten countries, who will receive power under the authority of Rome. This brings the entire description of greater Europe into the present century. On May 3rd 1948, the Council of Europe was established in London. The conference was attended by the Ten countries of Europe. On January 1st 1958, ten years later the European Economic Community or Common Market came into force. This European confederacy was established under the "Treaty of Rome".

The final clue is given in verse 3 of Revelation 13 when John describes one of the heads or countries of the beast, "wounded to death, and his deadly wound was healed". Here, John brings us to 1989 and what must be one of the most significant events of this century. After defeat at the end of World War II, Germany already economically, structurally and morally crippled suffered a further mortal wound to its ideology, as Germany was split into East and West. Since the 13th August 1961 the Berlin Wall had been a symbol of the Cold War, Communism versus Capitalism, Good versus Bad, East versus West, Christianity versus Atheism, the division of Germany's capital city symbolised the division of Europe.

However, the dramatic and unprecedented events of 1989 were to sensationally heal this mortal wound when, on the 9th November East Germany opened all its borders to the West. Within 24 hours the Berlin Wall was being demolished. The world stared on in wonder and amazement.

Having established that John is referring to Greater Europe, we then look at the next few verses and see that he is describing within these the power and domination of Europe over the last 2000 years.

> *And they worshipped the dragon which gave power unto the beast: and they worshipped the beast, saying, who is like unto the beast? Who is able to make war with him.*
> *And there was given unto him a mouth speaking great things and blasphemies: and power was given unto him to continue forty and two months.*
> Revelation 13. verses 4/5

Here John describes the league between the dragon, the Devil, and the beast, Greater Europe; its rise to power at the beginning of the 8th Century AD, the start of the Holy Roman Empire, through the Crusades and the Middle Ages, the Renaissance and the Reformation to the rise of the British

Empire, the French Revolution, culminating in the rival Imperial powers and the two great wars of the twentieth century. Once again, the huge power of Greater Europe and its dominance of the affairs of mankind are given a time scale of 42 months which, as we have seen in the earlier chapter "Judgement Day" corresponds to the 1260 years of Israel's scattering, between 688 AD and 1948.

The next 3 verses of Revelation 13 also describe the might, power and terrible destruction that Greater Europe had wrought on mankind during this period and in particular the persecution of believers, priests, clerics, rabbis and other righteous people as well as the huge power Greater Europe will have over all the peoples of the World.

> *And he opened his mouth in blasphemy against God, to blaspheme his name, and his tabernacle, and them that dwell in Heaven.*
> *And it was given unto him to make war with the saints, and to overcome them: and power was given him over all kindreds and tongues and nations.*
> *And all that dwell upon the earth shall worship him, whose names are not written in the book of life of the Lamb slain from the foundation of the world.*
> Revelation 13. verses 6/7/8

Having taken us from 688 AD to 1948, John in his vision then sees the future of Greater Europe from 1948 to the present day and beyond.

> *And I beheld another beast coming up out of the earth: and he had two horns like a lamb, and he spake as a dragon.*
> Revelation 13. verse 11

Here John sees another land mass coming out of the earth, but in the description of the beast as having "two horns like a lamb" he is telling us that this land mass or country is young like a lamb, a new country. John is describing the United States of America. America's huge influence over Europe and the rest of the world is detailed in the next verse.

> *And he exerciseth all the power of the first beast before him, and causeth the earth and them which dwell therein to worship the first beast, whose deadly wound was healed.*
> Revelation 13. verse 12

The enormous might and power of America, as displayed in World War II and latterly the Gulf War is described here, together with the enormous support America has given to Europe since the defeat of Germany in 1945. The next verse refers to the huge power of America's armoury and its ability to be all powerful with its nuclear and technological weapons.

> *And he doeth great wonders, so that he maketh fire come down from heaven on earth in the sight of men.*
> Revelation 13. verse 13

This verse in particular refers not only to the nuclear attacks on Hiroshima and Nagasaki, but to the immense arsenal of nuclear weapons and firepower at America's disposal; and let us not forget that so far, only America has used a nuclear weapon in anger.

The next verse describes America's huge influence over Europe, both financially and militaristically, and its imposition of capitalist ideology, the consumer society and the market forces that are now the butt of western civilisation.

> *And he deceiveth them that dwell on the earth, by means of those miracles which he had power to do in the sight of the beast; saying to them that dwell on the earth, that they should make an image to*

the beast, which had the wound by a sword, and did live.

Revelation 13. verse 14

In the last part of this verse we are given a clear reference to events that have already reached fruition. The setting up of the single European currency, the Euro, in 1999. The "image" referred to is the old biblical euphemism for money, and the following verse even appears to hint at the name of the currency most closely associated with this single European currency.

And he causeth all, both small and great, rich and poor, free and bond, to receive a mark in their right hand, or in their foreheads.

Revelation 13. verse 16.

Here, we are told that everyone will receive a "mark" in their right hand. Is John simply referring to a mark or blemish, a stamp or tattoo on everyone's right hand, or is he in some way trying to tell us that the European currency will be based on "The Mark" the currency of Germany. Is the description "in their foreheads" a reference to the already proposed single currency credit card and personal PIN number system. Further confirmation of the overall financial control this currency will have over the population as we move into the new millennium is then given in the next verse."

And that no man might buy or sell, save he that had the mark, or the name of the beast, or the number of his name.

Revelation 13. verse 17

This is a quite remarkable verse which made no sense until we reached the latter part of the twentieth century. The idea behind the single European currency, and indeed a single world currency, is control. The fact that "no man may buy or sell" is indicative of the control and the power over individuals that a single currency would have. We would all have our own personal number, no cash need be carried, not even a credit card because it is possible to implant a small microchip in the palm of the hand. This microchip would contain all our personal information and could be scanned in the same way that bar codes are now read in our supermarkets. Any person not having their own personal microchip and number would not be able to make any purchases, sell any goods or services or play any part in the economy. It is also of great interest to note that the bar codes themselves, without which the computerised western world would not be able to buy or sell, are composed of three sets of numbers, all calculated around the number six.

The description John is trying to convey is the power, might and control that Greater Europe, and latterly the United States of America, have held over the entire populations of the world over the past centuries, its cruel and inhuman acts and its forthcoming dominance of the world.

There is however, one further clue to be considered when looking for the true identity of the beast, and this is in the final verse of Revelation 13.

> *Here is wisdom. Let him that hath understanding count the number of the beast; for it is the number of a man; and his number is six hundred threescore and six.*
> Revelation 13. verse 18

As I mentioned at the beginning of this chapter, there have been many interpretations of the number 666. Some have ascribed it to the Antichrist himself, many others have used numerology, ciphers and cryptic anagrams to solve the mystery. However theology sometimes forgets that the Revelation was a simple straightforward message passed on to a simple straightforward man of the first century. Though John was undoubtedly an intelligent and deeply faithful man, he was not a complicated man, and so the many complicated theories surrounding the number must be dismissed. There is however, a far simpler solution which would have been immediately understood by John, a devout man who was well versed in the religious teachings of his time, both Christian and Judaic.

The number six is indeed the number of a man, but not one man.

> *So God created man in his own image.*
> *And the evening and the morning were the sixth day.*
>
> Genesis 1. verses 27/31

God created man and breathed his spirit into him on the sixth day. The number six is the number of mankind, the human race, and the triumvirate of the number six is a man attempting to imitate God, the three in one, the Father, the Son and the Holy Ghost, the Holy Trinity. The number 666 is a description of the unholy trinity, man turning away from God and thinking of himself as all powerful, with money and greed his gods and power and domination his goal.

Mankind has reached a crossroads. We have not regarded what created us, but rather have considered ourselves creators, herein lies our fault. For centuries people have tried to understand the meaning of the beast without reaching one simple conclusion - we are the beast!

Chapter 4
The Last Seven Plagues

And I saw another sign in heaven, great and marvellous, seven angels having the seven last plagues; for in them is filled up the wrath of God.
Revelation 15. verse 1

The beginning of the last seven plagues are already with us and clearly coincide with the events described in the last chapter "The Beast". Chapter 16 of Revelations gives us a chilling picture of natural disasters, pollution epidemic and war, the beginnings of which can already be seen in the world around us.

Indeed, the first two verses of the chapter immediately link themselves with Revelation Chapter 13, and the Beast.

And I heard a great voice out of the temple saying to the seven angels, Go your ways, and pour out the vials of the wrath of God upon the earth.
And the first went, and poured out his vial upon the earth; and there fell a noisome and grievous sore upon the men which had the mark of the beast, and upon them which worship his image.
Revelation 16. verses 1 & 2

As we have seen in the previous chapter the mark of the beast, and its image bring these verses immediately into the latter half of the 20th century and the consumer society. The line "noisome and grievous sore" seems to draw comparisons with the Great Plague of 1665, and implies that a plague will reach epidemic proportions towards the end of this century. There can only be one plague that this refers to. It is a disease that cannot be cured, and its spread throughout the world is now continuing at such a pace that it threatens the entire human race. The first of the last seven plagues is AIDS.

*And the second angel poured out his vial upon the
sea; and it became as the blood of a dead man:
and every living soul died in the sea.*
Revelation 16. verse 3

The pictures which flashed onto our television screens
towards the end of the Gulf War showing cormorants, their
feathers drenched in oil, slowly dying amidst the massive oil
pollution in the Gulf shocked the world. There is a
straightforward comparison between the colour of a sea
polluted by oil and the "blood of a dead man", both are a dirty
dark brown.

Recent reports from NASA's shuttle flights show that massive
pollution of the oceans is clearly visible from space, and the
dumping of chemical weapons, nuclear waste and hazardous
substances into our oceans over the last 45 years is now
giving great concern to environmentalists world wide. It would
seem that over the next few years we are going to reap the
whirlwind of a failed world environmental policy sown at the
end of the second world war. A policy that has seen the
industrial world dump its rubbish into our oceans totally
indiscriminately, without any regard for the fish and the
animals of the sea, and with no thought to the future of the
world. In continuing in this way the industrial world has had
only one motive in mind - profit!

*And the third angel poured out his vial upon the
rivers and the fountains of water, and they became
blood.*
Revelation 16. verse 4

Mankind has, since the industrial revolution of the 19th
century, had as much regard for the rivers of the world as for
the oceans. Indeed, the pollution of some of the world's major
rivers is now such that all life in them is dead, and humans too
would die should they drink the water. Not only are we
poisoning the rivers but as with our pollution of the oceans,

we are depriving ourselves of a valuable food source. How long will it be, as we continue our pollution, until the fish of the seas and rivers are either dead, or as in many parts of the world already unfit to eat.

And the fourth angel poured out his vial upon the sun; and power was given unto him to scorch men with fire.
And men were scorched with great heat, and blasphemed the name of God, which hath power over these plagues; and they repented not to give him glory.

Revelation 16. verses 8 & 9

Until a few years ago these two lines would perhaps have been difficult to interpret, but with the often reported problems of climatic change and ozone depletion making daily news headlines, the picture becomes all too clear.

Scientists and environmentalists, although not always in accord, agree that a depletion in the ozone layer will have dramatic changes not only on the climate, but on world population. There is already a hole in the ozone layer over Antarctica, and one of the consequences of this can be seen in Argentina. In the southern grasslands of the country where sheep farming is the major occupation, the sheep have developed cataracts and many thousands have gone blind. The shepherds have not only suffered similarly with cataracts, but a noticeable increase in melanoma, skin cancer amongst the shepherds has prompted the Argentine government to advise them to wear sun glasses and to cover exposed skin.

It is estimated that a 20% depletion of the ozone layer will cause a world wide epidemic of skin cancers, and with a massive depletion of the ozone layer currently taking place over the northern hemisphere, verses 8 and 9 predict that our worst fears will be realised. Climatic change will cause global warming on a huge scale, and the constant release of massive amounts of poisonous gasses into the atmosphere will deplete the ozone layer to a point where the ultra violet radiation reaching earth will become a major hazard, causing crop failure, blindness and such a huge epidemic of skin cancers that it will be considered dangerous to expose our skins to the sun. As horrific as this scenario seems, there is worse to come.

And the fifth angel poured out his vial upon the seat of the beast; and his kingdom was full of darkness; and they gnawed their tongues for pain.
Revelation 16. verse 10

The seat of the beast, as we have seen in the last chapter, is greater Europe and this verse predicts that this area will be covered in darkness. Whilst this seems not only highly improbable, but almost impossible, there is in our history a frightening precedent that should be a warning to us all. In 1159 BC, the volcano Hekla, on Iceland erupted in a massive explosion. This shows up in Irish tree rings of the period as being followed by twenty or so years of extremely low sunshine, and heavy rainfall, and it is thought that this darkness extended around much of the northern hemisphere. The effects were disastrous. Crops failed, famine ensued and in the following years of the Dark Ages the population of Europe was decimated.

In 1991 Mount Pinatubo erupted in the Philippines, and some ten months later NASA scientists, orbiting the earth in the shuttlecraft described how they could clearly see a dark cloud of particles above the northern hemisphere. Further evaluation of these particles proved they indeed came from the eruption of the Philippines volcano. It would seem that John, in verse ten of chapter sixteen foresees the after affects of one or possibly more massive volcanic eruptions in the near future and in the final part of the verse "they gnawed their tongues for pain" he sees the hunger caused by the famine that inevitably would follow. At present we cannot properly feed almost two thirds of the nearly six billion people living on this planet. Some estimates predict that by the end of the millennium the world's population will have almost doubled to ten billion, most of this growth coming from the third world countries.

Should there be a repeat of the Hekla eruption or something similar, the dust particles thrown into the atmosphere would not only do tremendous damage to the ozone layer, but would reflect sunlight away from the earth. The consequent result on the wheat producing areas of the American and Canadian mid-west, the Ukraine and Great Britain, the vegetable growing areas of northern Europe and America and the fruit growing areas of the Mediterranean, California and France would be totally devastating. Mankind would not be able to feed itself and the resultant chaos is almost too terrible to contemplate.

It is not only in the Bible that warnings are given about a coming world wide famine. The Book of Enoch, written around 100 BC, and taken out of the Canon by the church around 320 AD, has this chilling prediction in The Book of the Heavenly Luminaries.

> *2. And in the days of the sinners the years shall be shortened,*
> *And their seed shall be tardy on their lands and fields,*
> *And all things on earth shall alter,*
> *And shall not appear in their time:*
> *And the rain shall be kept back*
> *And the heaven shall withhold it.*
> *3. And in those times the fruits of the earth shall be backward,*
> *And shall not grow in their time,*
> *And the fruits of the trees shall be withheld in their time.*
>
> 2 Enoch. Chapter 80. Verses 2 & 3

The Book of Enoch is probably the most notable apocalyptic work outside the canonical scriptures and in the preceding verses it appears that climatic changes will bring on this approaching famine. As we are now beginning to realise, global warming, the greenhouse affect and the depletion of the ozone layer are already starting to change the world's weather.

The climate of the earth is extremely finely balanced. Most crops, fruits and vegetables need very specific amounts of sunshine and rainfall in order to grow. Any small change in the amount of sunlight and rainfall in certain areas of the world would be disastrous, causing crop failure on a massive scale, and leading to hunger and starvation on a world wide level never before experienced.

> *And the sixth angel poured out his vial upon the great river Euphrates; and the water thereof was dried up, that the way of the kings of the east might be prepared.*
>
> Revelation 16. verse 12

This, the penultimate plague, starts by immediately identifying not only the area, but the geographical feature that will be affected. The river Euphrates runs through what was once Mesopotamia, the supposed site of the Garden of Eden. It is the largest river in South West Asia, rising in the foothills of north east Turkey fairly near Mount Ararat. It then flows almost 3,000 kilometres south through Turkey, Syria and Iraq, finally disgorging itself into the Gulf through the Shatt-al Arab waterway.

During the Gulf War there was a suggestion that the Euphrates could be stopped from flowing through Iraq by closing the Ataturk Dam, built in 1981. This however was not done, as South West Asia's other great river the Tigris, rising in the Taurus mountains of Southern Turkey and running parallel and to the east of the Euphrates through Iraq has no dams on the river, and is well able to supply the demands of Baghdad and the rest of Iraq. However, the fact remains that since the building of the Ataturk Dam, it is possible to dry up the flow of the great River Euphrates. Whether the prediction in verse 12 refers to a man made event that leads to the drying up of the Euphrates or a natural disaster is unclear. Since the end of the Gulf War, Iraq has embarked on a campaign against the Marsh Arabs that has involved the draining of the marshes in the Euphrates basin in south west Iraq. Perhaps Saddam Hussein is already beginning to fulfil this prophecy, preparing the way for the "Kings of the East". Who these kings of the east are can at present only be surmised at, but events over the last few years seem to point in only one direction. Directly to the east of the Euphrates is Iraq, and further east the old Persian empire, now modern day Iran. Further east still, brings us to Afghanistan and Pakistan and onwards over the Himalayas to China. In the last few years we have seen a steady rise of fundamental Islam in the countries to the east of the Euphrates. True, many of these fundamentalists are in opposition to other Muslim groups within their countries, but there is one thing that more than anything else unites every Muslim under Islam. It is the belief that the West, America and Europe, together with Christianity and Judaism have for hundreds of years oppressed Islam. This perception has been so strongly reinforced during the events of the last thirty years that many Muslims now see a Jihad, or Holy War, against the West as an inevitability. Could it be that in the last part of verse 12 John has seen the beginnings of a Muslim invasion of the West.

And I saw three unclean spirits like frogs come out of the mouth of the dragon, and out of the mouth of the beast, and out of the mouth of the false prophet.

Revelation 16. verse 13

Once again, in a verse still associated with the sixth plague John sees the rise of three personalities from the Dragon, America; The Beast, Greater Europe; and the false prophet. This is the first time the false prophet is mentioned, but as it would appear to be connected with verse 12 and the drying up of the Euphrates, it seems that John see the rise of three great leaders, one from America, one from Greater Europe and one from the world of Islam. What these three leaders intentions are is made abundantly clear in the next verse.

For they are the spirits of devils, working miracles, which go forth unto the kings of the earth and the whole world, to gather them to the battle of that great day of God Almighty.
Revelation 16. verse 14

The intention of these three leaders is made with precise clarity in this verse. The American, Greater European and Muslim leaders will draw the world into its final conflict.

And he gathered them together into a place called in the Hebrew tongue Armageddon.
Revelation 16. verse 16

There has been much speculation about the location of Armageddon. Many have said it refers to a valley in northern Israel close to its border with Syria, whilst others have believed it to be the Bekka valley, further to the east. It is impossible to say with any certainty the precise location of Armageddon, indeed it may not be a place in the standard sense, as some people have translated Armageddon simply as "the final conflict". Whatever the truth, the events that follow are apocalyptic.

And the seventh angel poured out his vial into the air; and there came a great voice out of the temple of heaven, from the throne, saying it is done.
And there were voices, and thunders, and

lightnings; and there was a great earthquake, such as was not since men were upon the earth, so mighty an earthquake, and so great.
                              Revelation 16. verses 17 & 18

So now we have reached the last of the plagues, the final seventh plague. The thunders and lightnings could be synonymous with aerial and nuclear warfare, or massive storms around the world, but the description of the earthquake is quite conclusive. The phrase "such as was not since men were upon earth" means quite simply the most powerful earthquake ever. So powerful is this earthquake that it reeks devastation on a world wide scale never before seen.

And the great city was divided into three parts, and the cities of the nations fell; and great Babylon came in remembrance before God, to give unto her the cup of the wine of the fierceness of his wrath.
                              Revelation 16. verse 19

Scientists now point to the inevitability of a severe earthquake along the San Andreas fault in the near future, and recently it has become evident that the movement of the Pacific plate will not only have dire consequences for the state of California, but at its western end, the Pacific plate runs through New Zealand, Australia and northwards to Japan. Many scientists now agree that the Californian earthquake when it comes, will not only reek havoc along America's west coast but would have a disastrous effect in New Zealand and would hit Japan with such force that the islands of Honshu and Hokkaido would be totally devastated. The Revelation is not the only place where one finds prophecies concerning earthquakes. In the book of Matthew, Jesus is asked by his disciples on the Mount of Olives to tell them about the end of the world, and the sign of his second coming.

For nation shall rise against nation, and kingdom against kingdom, and there shall be famines, and pestilences, and earthquakes, in divers places.
Matthew 24. verse 7

Nostradamus also predicts a great earthquake in two quatrains, and in one of these gives a very precise dating.

Sol vingt de taurus si fort terre trembler.
Le grand theatre rempli ruinera,
L'air ciel & terre obscurcir & troubler
Lors l'infidelle Dieu & sainctz voguera.

The sun in twenty degrees of Taurus there is a great earthquake.
The great theatre filled up and ruined,
The air, sky and land will be dark and troubled,
Then the unbeliever will call on God and the saints.
Century 9. Quatrain 83

As each of the twelve sun signs covers a period of 30 days, and there are 360 degrees in a circle; then each day is one degree. The sun enters Taurus on April 21st and therefore 20 degrees of Taurus is 20 days later. In this way Nostradamus has given us the date of May 10th for this great earthquake. In the second line the words "Le grand theatre" are hard to explain. Could it be however, that this is Nostradamus' way of describing Hollywood, the movie making capital of the world, with its huge sound stages and enormous studios. To a man in the 16th Century, Hollywood surely could be described as "the great theatre".

The reference to the air, sky and land being dark and troubled seems to evoke a picture of a terrible calamity on earth involving not only a great earthquake, but also a cataclysmic series of volcanic and meteorological activities that have never before been seen on earth. This invokes a response from *"l'infidelle"* or unbeliever who, despite the belief in his own power, calls upon God and the Saints for help. By this time, it is too late.

Le tremblement si fort au mois de May,
Saturne, Caper, Jupiter, Mercure au beuf:
Venus aussi Cancer, Mars, en Nonnay,
Tombera gresse lors plus grosse qu'un euf.

A very strong earthquake in the month of May,
Saturn in Capricorn, Jupiter and Mercury in Taurus:
Venus also in Cancer, Mars in Virgo,
Then hail will fall, greater than an egg.

Century 10. Quatrain 67

This astrological accumulation of planets in the zodiac is rare indeed, but again it points to a major earthquake in the month of May, and appears to be followed by a bombardment of the planet by a hail of rocks. Could this be an after effect of volcanic action, or is this the aftermath of a passing of a huge comet, of which I will talk later. Whatever the answer is to this question, the next verse of Revelation is very succinct in its description of what follows.

And every island fled away, and the mountains were not found.

Revelation 16. verse 20

Recently geologists have discovered that the world's tectonic plates, that part of the earth's crust that the continents are built on, are not only moving against each other, but are extremely fluid. Geologists now believe that because of this the world's greatest mountain range, the Himalayas, could one day collapse under its own weight.

The Himalayas which are fold mountains were formed when the continental plates of India and Asia collided. The earthquake that is described in Revelation could be of such a magnitude that not only the Pacific plate is affected, but there could be a major "knock on" effect, causing the two other great fault lines, the African rift valley running from South Africa through to the Mediterranean, and the Mid Atlantic Ridge to split asunder. Should this happen then Revelation 16 verse 20 would certainly become a reality. Once again it is not only Revelation that speaks of these things.

The great prophet Mohammed, speaking in the name of God, the Compassionate, the Merciful, says in the Koran;

> *The day cometh when the earth and the*
> *mountains shall be shaken, and the mountains*
> *shall become a loose sand heap.*
>
> Koran. Sura 73. verse 14

The book of Enoch also has this warning in the "Parable of Enoch on the future lot of the Wicked and the Righteous".

> *And the high mountains shall be shaken*
> *And the high hills shall be made low*
> *And shall melt like wax before the flame*
> *And the earth shall be wholly rent in sunder*
> *And all that is upon the earth shall perish*
> *And there shall be a judgement upon all.*
>
> 1 Enoch. verses 6 – 7

The final verse of Revelation 16 describes an event similar to a previous Nostradamus quatrain concerning the earthquake in May.

> *And there fell upon men a great hail out of*
> *heaven, every stone about the weight of a talent:*
> *and men blasphemed God because of the plague*
> *of the hail; for the plague thereof was exceeding*
> *great.*
>
> Revelation 16. verse 21

As mentioned earlier in this chapter, this could be the result of a massive volcanic eruption, or perhaps the results of a comet passing close to the earth. The appearance of a huge comet is mentioned frequently in Nostradamus, and will be dealt with in a future chapter. One thing is however, certain. The last seven plagues are a combination of man-made and natural disasters, concerning our pollution of the planet, man's desire to decimate his neighbour, and natural events we have no control over. There is also one other conclusion we can reach concerning the last seven plagues. They are here now.

Chapter 5
The Vatican and the Papacy

*And there came one of the seven angels which
had the seven vials, and talked with me, saying
unto me, Come hither; I will show unto thee the
judgement of the great whore that sitteth upon
many waters:*

Revelation 17. Verse 1

Chapter 17 of the Book of Revelation is probably one of the
most contentious chapters anywhere in the Bible. The reason
for this is simple. The eighteen verses of Revelation chapter
seventeen contain within them a graphic description of the
power, corruption and final collapse of the Roman Catholic
Church. To most Christians naturally this is anathema.
However it is not only in the Bible that we find predictions of
the fall of the Catholic Church.

First, though we must look closely at chapter seventeen of the
Book of Revelation. Saint John, like the other Biblical
prophets who received visions of the future, was first shown
a vision and then afterwards given an understanding of the
things he had been shown. The visions first, the
interpretation second.

*So he carried me away in the spirit into the
wilderness: and I saw a woman sit upon a scarlet
coloured beast, full of names of blasphemy, having
seven heads and ten horns.*

Revelation 17. Verse 3

This is not the first time the seven heads and ten horns have
been mentioned in the Bible, or indeed in this book. The
seven heads refer to the city of Rome, the ten horns to
Europe, as we have seen in Chapter 3, but what of the
woman, the great whore.

And the woman was arrayed in purple and scarlet colour, and decked with gold and precious stones and pearls, having a golden cup in her hand full of abominations and filthiness of her fornications.
                                    Revelation 17. Verse 4

This to me is one of the most descriptive verses anywhere in the Bible, so much so that I'm amazed it was not removed by the Church, for it describes with startling accuracy the beginning of the Roman Catholic Mass, the priest dressed in scarlet and purple robes, wearing his gold and be-jewelled sashes of authority, his arms raised above his head, a golden chalice in his hands. When one is elevated to the position of Cardinal in the Roman Catholic Church it is known as "taking the purple". As if to confirm this description, the verse that follows contains within it yet another important reference to the Roman Catholic Church, a reference that caused the Vatican severe embarrassment some one thousand years ago.

And upon her forehead was a name written, MYSTERY, BABYLON THE GREAT, THE MOTHER OF HARLOTS AND ABOMINATIONS OF THE EARTH.
                                    Revelation 17. Verse 5

Until the 12th Century the Papal Tiara, a three cornered or Tricorn hat with three crowns placed atop the three points, had the word MYSTERIUM, Latin for mystery written across the front of the headband, directly across the Pope's forehead. At some point in the 12th Century the word was removed. Throughout the Book of Revelation academics and theologians agree that Babylon refers specifically to Rome. Once again the reference to the Papacy and the Roman Catholic Church is unequivocal.

Now that Saint John has been shown the vision, he is then given its interpretation.

And the angel said unto me, Wherefore didst thou marvel? I will tell you the mystery of the woman, and of the beast that carrieth her, which hath seven heads and ten horns.

And here is the mind which hath wisdom. The seven heads are seven mountains, on which the woman sitteth.

Revelation 17. Verses 7 & 9

Again this is a clear reference to the city of Rome, standing as it does on seven hills. The next interpretation refers directly back to verse one of chapter seventeen and the "great whore that sitteth upon many waters".

And he saith unto me, The waters which thou sawest, where the whore sitteth, are peoples, and multitudes, and nations and tongues.

Revelation 17. Verse 15

In this verse the interpretation of the "waters" clearly indicates the almost one billion Catholics around the world, ruled over by the Vatican and the Papacy. The final verse of chapter seventeen is incontrovertible in its description of the Vatican, the seat of the Roman Catholic Church within the eternal city of Rome.

And the woman which thou sawest is that great city, which reigneth over the Kings of the earth.

Revelation 17. Verse 18

Here then in Chapter seventeen of the Book of Revelation we see a description of the Roman Catholic Church and included within the chapter is the fate not only of the Church but of the City of Rome itself.

And the ten horns which thou sawest upon the beast, these shall hate the whore, and shall make her desolate and naked, and shall eat her flesh, and burn her with fire.

Revelation 17. Verse 16

As explained in Chapter 3 The Beast, the ten horns represent the ten countries of Europe, now combined into the European Union. Though the total destruction of Rome seems highly unlikely the Bible is not the only place where this cataclysmic event is forecast, as well as the collapse of both the Papacy and the Roman Catholic Church.

The Twelfth Magic Figure of Paracelsus shows in the accompanying figure the chair of Saint Peter upside down, followed by the following prognostication.

> *Although one may seat himself securely, yet there is no chair that may not fall, and also he that sitteth thereon. And thou seatest thyself upon this chair but thou shouldst not be thereon. Thou shouldst be below and not above. For thou art a burthen and an unbearable yoke, therefore falls S.P. Thou hast seated thyself thereon and he hath paid thee and given thee the reward thou was seeking: Temporal honour and praise: and these thou hast gathered all together in thyself and swallowed them up. Therefore as a temporal thing thou must also pass away.*
>
> Paracelsus. The Twelfth Magic Figure

This figure clearly foreshadows the final and complete collapse of the Papacy and is followed in the Thirtieth Magic Figure, which shows a monk, preacher and mystic seated together, with a similar prediction.

> *Thou hast often assembled, and much congregated, but the enemy was not with thee, therefore all things thou hast resolved were to no purpose and in vain. It must be alone that thou wilt forgo thy claims, and reflect of whom thou art, whom thou hast learnt, and what thou wouldst do if thou wert to turn aside, and wouldst acknowledge thyself and others; then wouldst thou*

cease. But as thou desirest to be what thou shouldst not be, and wilt sit upon the chair of Saint Peter, and whereas the same must fall; therefore thou mayest not continue in thy plots, for he shall turn aside thy design who is thy master.

Paracelsus. The thirtieth Magic Figure

In this figure it appears Paracelsus is not only prophesying the fall of the Papacy but of the entire Roman Catholic Church. As if to strengthen this description the Elucidation of the Prognostication for the Twelfth Magic Figure states;

It is a great thing that the Virgin Mary has spoken, that He has deposed the mighty ones from the chair. Therefore let no one marvel that impossible things come to pass, for these are in the hand of God.

So we now have both the Bible and Paracelsus predicting the fall of the Church of Rome, but Nostradamus is even more specific in his predictions naming not only Rome and the Catholic Church but alluding in a series of quatrains to Pope John Paul II, giving the time and place of his death. As mentioned in Chapter I, The Prophets and the Prophecies, Nostradamus uses a convolution of Malachy's epithet for John Paul II. Malachy's epithet "De Labore Solis" or "work of the sun" is transformed by Nostradamus into a two word description that not only fits Malachy's epithet exactly, but also gives the Pope's name and his birthplace.

Pol mensolee mourra trois lieus du Rosne
Fuis les deux prochains tarasc destrois:
Car Mars fera le plus horrible trosne,
De coq & d'aigle de France, freres trois.

"Polish Paul" the work of the sun will die three leagues from the Rhone,
Having fled between the two rocks of Tarascon

(and Beaucaire)
Then war will take up its horrible throne,
Of the Cock and the Eagle and the three brothers
of France.
Century 8. Quatrain 46

The first line identifies John Paul II as "the work of the sun" and states he will die in France at a distance of three leagues from the river Rhone. The two towns of Tarascon and Beaucaire sit atop two hills either side of the River Rhone south of Avignon in Provence, France. The third line is self explanatory and the last line of the quatrain could have several meanings. It could for example refer to France, the cockerel being one of France's emblems and the eagle signifying the United States of America, but what of the three brothers of France? This could apply equally to any of France's European partners such as the United Kingdom, Germany and Italy, or the other three members of the United Nations Security Council that sit with France and America, namely Russia, China and once more the UK. Though the last three lines of this quatrain are somewhat obscure, line one is very definite about where John Paul II will die.

Salon, Mansol, Tarascon de SEX. l'arc,
Ou est debout encor la piramide:
Viendront livrer le Prince Dannemarc,
Rachat honni au temple d'Artemide.

Salon, The work of the sun, Tarascon, Aix en Provence, Monaco,
Where the pyramid again stands,
They will come to deliver the Prince of Dannemarc,
The redeemer honoured at the temple of Artemis.
Century 4. Quatrain 27

Two things are immediately clear in line one of this quatrain, firstly the use by Nostradamus of "Mansol" indicating John Paul II and the mention once again of Tarascon. The other places mentioned are all in Provence, southern France, the word SEX signifying Aquae Sextiae, the Roman name for Aix en Provence and l'arc signifying ARX Monoeci, the Roman name for Monaco. So from line one it appears that once again John Paul II is placed in France. This is further confirmed by line two with the pyramid referring to the now famous glass pyramid standing outside the Louvre in Paris.

Line three of this quatrain is a typically obscure Nostradamus place name. Two interpretations can be put forward to identify the "Prince Dannemarc". Firstly that the word "Dannemarc" implies Denmark, however this then begs the question "who is the Prince of Denmark"? In Literary terms this can only be Hamlet, Shakespeare's tragic Prince Hal of Denmark. The word "livrer" in this line, translated as deliver could well imply actors delivering their lines. Perhaps this line indicates a Papal visit to a performance of Hamlet at the theatre somewhere in France.

The other possible explanation of this line is that it should have read "Prince D'Annemarc" and that Annemarc is a convoluted anagram of America. Using this interpretation it appears that Nostradamus is indicating the President of the United States and once again the word "livrer" could signify the four yearly electoral process by which America's president is elected. Although America goes to the polls in November every fourth year the razzmatazz of the campaign trail starts many months before that, culminating in the frenzied electioneering of September and October as the respective candidates vie for the votes of the American public.

Though both of these interpretations could be correct, we still have line four to contend with. The word "Rachat" comes from the old French word Rachatere meaning redeemer or saviour. That the redeemer should be honoured at the temple of Artemis however, is somewhat incongruous. The temple of Artemis would seem to refer to the most famous temple of that name at Ephesus, situated in the west of modern day Turkey. However, Artemis was a Greek Goddess whose Roman equivalent was Diana. That the redeemer Jesus Christ, should be honoured in modern day Turkey, an Islamic nation seems somewhat improbable, however if we take the Roman equivalent of Artemis, then it seems quite conceivable that a Christian ceremony, possibly a Roman Catholic Mass could be held at a church or cathedral dedicated to Diana.

Although this quatrain is typically obscure and hard to interpret, it once again places John Paul II in France. He has visited France many times during his Papacy, the last times being in August 1997 and September 1996.

> *De Pol MANSOL dans caverne caprine*
> *Cache & prins extrait hors par la barbe,*
> *Capitif mene comme beste mastine*
> *Par Begourdans amenee pres de Tarbe.*

Of Polish Paul the work of the sun in a goats cave
Hidden and taken pulled out by the barbarians,
Captives led like dogs
By the Begourdans brought close to Tarbes.
Century 10. Quatrain 29

The word "caprine" in line one is a Latin adjective that means "appertaining to goats" whilst the words "beste mastine" in line three refer to a mastiff dog. The last line places John Paul II in France once again, as Tarbes is the chief city of the Bigorre region of southern France, close to the Catholic holy site of Lourdes. A fascinating quatrain but again, other than the fact that it places John Paul II in France possibly at Lourdes, the full meaning is as usual, hard to grasp. What does seem clear from the preceding quatrains is that John Paul II will undertake a journey to the south of France, passing down the Rhone valley through Avignon home of the Papacy during the Babylonian captivity of 1309 - 1378 and then southward between the towns of Tarascon and Beaucaine to Lourdes. For John Paul II this would be a classic pilgrimage, but Nostradamus seems to infer that this will be the Pope's final journey.

In chapter one I refer to the last two Popes following John Paul II. The next Pope has Saint Malachy's epithet "Gloria Olivae" - the glory of the olive. This could have many meanings but the two most likely are that the next Pope will either be a Benedictine cardinal, the Benedictines are also known as Olivetans, or come from the Tuscany region of Italy, famous for its olive oil. The most senior Benedictine cardinal in the Vatican was Cardinal Basil Hume, who sadly died last year, so we must look elsewhere. Taking the Tuscany region as the "home" of Italian olive oil, perhaps the next Pontiff will be a native of that region, or perhaps an Archbishop of Florence. Interestingly enough, the present Archbishop of Florence was not only born just outside that beautiful city, but his name is Silvano Piovanelli. The word "Olivae" can be taken directly from his surname. Was Malachy cunning enough to have given this as a major clue to the identity of the next Pope? Time will tell, but in January 2000 I wrote an article about my findings and sent it to various newspapers in the hope that they might be interested in publishing my thoughts. Amongst the newspapers who received it but turned it down were The Times, The New York Times, The Catholic Herald and The Catholic World News. Here is the final paragraph :-

*"Saint Malachy has, thus far, correctly identified every Pope since 1143. The next Pope has the epithet "Gloria Olivae"..............The Glory of the Olive.There has been much speculation over the years as to who this epithet may refer to. In my book **"The Cassandra Prophecy"** I give various possible explanations, one of which I now believe to be correct. Tuscanny is famous as the most important olive growing region in Italy, it's capital is Florence. The current Archbishop of Florence was born in 1924 in Ronta di Mugello*

*near Florence. His father was an olive grower.   The Archbishop's name is Silvano Piovanelli. You can extract the word "**Olivae**" from the surname "**Piovanelli**" Is this St. Malachy's "Gloria Olivae" or just a simple coincidence?*

There are two more quatrains worth noting concerning the Papacy and both of these talk of an event that appears not to have happened to date.

> *La grand estoille par sept jours brulera,*
> *Nuee fera deux soleils apparoir:*
> *Le gros mastin toute nuict hurlera.*
> *Quand grand pontife changera de terroir.*

> The great star/comet will blaze for seven days,
> The sky will appear to have two suns:
> The British leader/great dog will howl all night,
> When the great Pontiff changes countries.
>   Century 2. Quatrain 41

That a great star or comet will shine for only seven days and be of such size and brightness as to equal the sun seems inconceivable and has certainly not occurred since Nostradamus published his quatrains. Line three is interesting in so far as another name for a mastiff in French is "le dogue anglais", so it could well refer to a great Englishman. The Papacy as mentioned earlier, last changed countries during the Babylonian captivity in the 14th century. There is one other interesting quatrain that deals with the Papacy and a comet.

> *Apparoistra vers la Septentrion,*
> *Non loin de Cancer l'estoille chevelue:*
> *Suze, Sienne, Boece, Eretrion,*
> *Mourra de Rome grand, la nuict disperue.*
> Appearing close to Ursa Major,
> Shortly after June 21, the comet:
> Suse, Sienne, Greece and the Red Sea,

The great Pope of Rome will die, the night the comet disappears.

Century 6. Quatrain 6

The word Septentrion in the first line is from the Latin septentrio, the seven star constellation near the Pole star, known as Ursa Major or the great bear. In line two a dating is given, the sun entering Cancer on June 21st. Suse and Sienne are towns in France, although with typical Nostradamus ambiguity he could be referring to Susa and Sienna, both in Italy. Boece is the Boeotia region of ancient Greece and Eretrion refers to the Erythraeum mare, the Red Sea. That a comet should disappear seems strange as they normally fade from the sky, and which Pope this quatrain refers to is impossible to say. However this event does not appear to have happened since Nostradamus published his quatrains in 1555.

As mentioned previously according to Saint Malachy the Pope who follows "Gloria Olivae" will be the last Pope of the Roman Catholic Church, his predictions finishing with this short but fascinating prophecy.

> *In the final persecution of the Holy Roman Church there will reign Peter the Roman, who will feed his flock among many tribulations, after which the seven hilled city will be destroyed and the dreadful Judge will judge the people.*

That the Catholic Church and Rome itself should be destroyed must seem completely impossible for many people, particularly those of the Roman Catholic faith, however it is worth once again considering the words of Paracelsus in his elucidation of the prognostication contained in the Twelfth Magic Figure.

> *Therefore let no one marvel that impossible things come to pass, for those are in the hands of God.*
Paracelsus. The Twelfth Magic Figure

Chapter 6
The Eclipse, The Alignment and the Grand Cross

And there shall be signs in the sun, and in the moon, and in the stars

St. Luke 21. Verse 25

In many of the ancient writings there are prophecies of signs in the sky coming as warnings to mankind that the end times, the "latter days" are here. Between now and the start of the new millennium we will indeed see "signs in the sky". Whether or not these signs are the portents of a coming global catastrophe as predicted, remains to be seen. One thing however is clear, as the century renews itself a series of astronomical events will occur that could have a profound effect on the future of mankind and the planet.

Then the Sun, Moon and Stars shall appear as signs that have to be considered. The end however is not yet, although there are signs thereof, but the calamity is only beginning.

Preface to the Prognostications of Paracelsus

On August 11th 1999 the world witnessed the final total eclipse of the millennium. It began at sunrise 400 miles off the coast of Nova Scotia, crossing the Atlantic to reach the southern tip of the United Kingdom at approximately 10.00 in the morning Greenwich Mean Time. It then passed over northern France, Europe, The Black Sea and Turkey to cross Syria, Iraq, Iran, Pakistan and northern India ending at sunset over the Bay of Bengal.

For thousands of years eclipses have been regarded by many people as harbingers of disaster. It is interesting to note that Operation Desert Storm, starting as it did on January 15th 1991 was begun during a total eclipse of the sun. This particular eclipse however, differed from others in one very specific way. The total eclipse of August 11th 1999 activated a most extraordinary astronomical phenomenon, a Grand Cross of planets in the sky with the four corners of the cross in the fixed signs of Leo, Taurus, Scorpio and Aquarius, the four signs which correspond with the four beasts of the Apocalypse in the Book of Revelation. This dramatic event occurred on August 18th 1999, exactly seven days after the final total eclipse of the millennium.

Interestingly, in between these two events, which some scientists pronounced would have a gravitational effect on the earth, a huge earthquake in Turkey killed almost 20,000 people. Where the eclipse and the grand cross warnings to the world of a coming catastrophe?

These two remarkable astronomical events could in some way be linked with one of the very few dated quatrains of Nostradamus. Century 10, quatrain 72 is one of the French seer's most famous predictions saying as it does that:-

In the year 1999 seven months
From the sky will come a great king of terror.
Resurrecting the ancient king of the Mongols,
Before and after war reigns happily.
                              Century 10. Quatrain 72

It could be suggested that Nostradamus is in fact predicting the forthcoming total eclipse, the second line of the quatrain alluding to the inherent fear of total eclipses during the middle ages. However, Nostradamus was an extremely competent astronomer and it is doubtful he would make such a mistake. If it is not a reference to the eclipse, it could well describe some form of aerial warfare which stirs up trouble within ancient Mongolia comprising as it does of southern China, the central Asian states of the former Soviet Union and Afghanistan.

The quatrain itself is typically ambiguous with regard to the date specified. Because there is no conjunction between the year and the months it is almost impossible to know the exact date Nostradamus is trying to convey. Most commentators interpret the date as being July of 1999, assuming that Nostradamus simply left out the conjunction "et" meaning "and". This leaves us with a problem. Nothing remotely like the events described in the quatrain occurred in July 1999. Could Nostradamus then have meant us to interpret the prophecy as being literally the full year of 1999, plus seven months, which would bring us to July 2000. Time alone will tell, but it is just possible the prediction has already been fulfilled. If Nostradamus meant the quatrain to be interpreted as the year 1999, with seven months left in the year, in other words May 1999, we find an interesting coincidence. On May 6th. the Chinese embassy in Belgrade was accidentally hit by cruise missiles during the Kosovo crisis, destroying the embassy and killing several Chinese embassy workers. The reaction to this event in China was one of considerable anger, with American embassies and government buildings targeted in violent anti-American demonstrations. Looking again at the quatrain, could a cruise missile be described as a "King of terror" coming as it does, from the skies. Could the unrest this event generated in China be interpreted as a "bringing back to life" of the spirit of Genghis Khan, the great leader of the Mongols. Considering the last line of the quatrain, the war in Kosovo continued for some time after this event so war did indeed reign "before and after" this event.

Nostradamus has a similar rather gloomy prediction concerning signs in the sky that appear at the turn of the millennium.

> *After great misery for mankind, an even greater misery appears,*
> *The great cycle of the centuries is renewed:*
> *It will rain blood, milk, famine, fire and disease,*
> *In the sky will be seen a fire, dragging a trail of sparks*
> Century 2. Quatrain 46

The second line refers directly to the change from one millennium to another. As Nostradamus published his quatrains in 1555, he could only be referring to this millennium. The last line is somewhat ambiguous and could be describing a comet in the sky equally as well as some form of missile or rocket. Looked at in the context of the rest of the quatrain however, it seems more likely to be the latter.

The Bible contains many references to signs appearing in the sky as warnings to the world's population. One in particular, spoken by Jesus Christ to his disciples is of particular significance for one reason. The phrase appears in the gospels of Matthew, Mark and Luke.

Immediately after the tribulation of those days shall the sun be darkened, and the moon shall not give her light, and the stars shall fall from heaven, and the power of the heavens shall be shaken.

St. Matthew 24. Verse 29

And the stars of heaven shall fall, and the powers that are in heaven shall be shaken.

St. Mark 13. Verse 25

Men's hearts failing them for fear, and for looking after those things which are coming on the earth: for the powers of heaven shall be shaken.

St. Luke 21. Verse26

To gain the full significance of these three verses, it is necessary to look at how the original texts of the gospels were written. The language of the apostles writing these texts was Greek, indeed the Old Testament containing 39 books was written mainly in Hebrew, with some Aramaic, but first collected together and translated into Greek in the third century BC. This was known as the Septuagint Old Testament.

The writings of the New Testament were collected together in the second century AD in the original Greek and not until the fourth century AD did the Latin or Vulgate Bible appear.

The three verses mentioned previously all refer to the "power of the heavens being shaken". Taken literally this seems to be an event that is hard to understand. Mention of the sun and moon being darkened could be explained in many ways. Pollution spreading into the atmosphere or volcanic eruptions could cause just such an effect. As could a nuclear war. That the "heavens could be shaken" however seems extraordinary until you look at the original Greek text. The word for the "heavens" in Greek is "ouranus". Herschel took this word in March 1781 to name his newly discovered planet Uranus. Eight years later in 1789, a mining engineer discovered a white metal shining out from the black rock-face he was cutting. He thought the white metal particles looked like the stars in the heavens. The mining engineer was named Klaproth, the metal element he had discovered he called Uranium.

Is the real message contained in the writings of Matthew, Mark and Luke that the "power of uranium shall be shaken". In this context it could mean only one thing - nuclear war. There are two similar verses in the Old Testament book of the prophet Joel. These also refer to signs in the sky.

> *The sun shall be turned into darkness, and the moon into blood, before the great and terrible day of the Lord come.*
> Joel 2. Verse 31
> *The sun and the moon shall be darkened, and the stars shall withdraw their shining.*
> Joel 3. Verse 15

The ambiguity of these two verses is obvious. It could refer to the result of volcanic eruptions just as easily as it could to a total eclipse of the sun, the stars shining in the sky during totality and gradually fading as the sun reappears. It is a fact that half a billion people in the world live near volcanoes. During the last ten years volcanic activity around the globe has increased dramatically. Geologists are currently monitoring three new volcanoes in Europe, one some ten miles north of Rome, a second, the biggest of its kind in Europe, on the bed of the Tyrrhenian Sea off the southern coast of Italy, and the third forming on the seabed north of the island of Crete.

There are certain astronomical events that many scientists believe increase volcanic and earthquake activity around the world. One of these is the increase in solar activity and sun spots. At the beginning of this new millennium the sun reached what astronomers call the "solar maximum", the high point in the sun's solar cycle. At this time there was a great deal of sun spot activity and an increase in solar flares. These solar flares generate enormous electromagnetic energy that extends far past earth into space, the fluctuating particle streams and magnetic fields interacting with earth's atmosphere to cause auroras and huge magnetic storms. The increase in volcanic activity as we move into the new millennium could, in part, be due to this extraordinary event.

Another rare astronomical situation occurred on May 5th. 2000 when we witnessed an alignment of the planets, with the earth on one side of the sun and directly opposite on the other side of the sun, the planets Mercury, Venus, Mars, Jupiter and Saturn are aligned together. Uranus and Neptune form a 90 degree angle to this alignment. Although this appeared to have no effect whatsoever on the planet, it is true to say that we are seeing an increase in earthquake and volcanic activity around the world.

We have seen major earthquakes in Greece, Taiwan, the United States, Turkey and on the Pacific islands of Vanuatu, and volcanic activity in the world, not only in Guyana, Japan, the Philippines, Indonesia and Iceland, but around Mt. Etna and Mt. Versuvius in Europe is rapidly increasing. Geologists point to the fact that the fault line that stretches from the tip of Africa through the "Rift Valley" and northwards through the Mediterranean and across Turkey is moving, and more earthquakes are anticipated

But what of these "signs in the sky" which are predicted. What affect will they eventually have on the planet. If the eclipse, the grand cross and the alignment are warnings to us, what else can we expect to happen? Are there any more signs to contemplate? Perhaps so, and one event could well be caused by a man made object.

There is amongst the satellites that orbit the earth, one that is very different to all the others. Its main difference is its size. The Russian MIR space station is massive, weighing some 140 tons. Towards the end of 1999 the last cosmonaut left the space station and its booster rockets were fired for the last time to begin a process that will see it re-enter the earth's atmosphere at some 17,500 miles per hour. The scientists hope that as MIR descends it will break into five major components which will burn up. However, these components weigh some twenty tons each and the possibility of one of them reaching the surface of the earth is high. Nostradamus has an intriguing quatrain which appears to identify quite specifically a Russian satellite.

Si grand Famine par unde pestifere.
Par pluie longue le long du polle arctique,
Samorobin cent lieux de l'hemisphere,
Vivront sans loi exempt de pollitique.

So great a famine by a wave of pestilence.
Through its long rain the length of the arctic pole,
The self operated thing one hundred leagues above the hemisphere,
They will live without law, exempt from politics.

Century 6. Quatrain 5

The key word in this quatrain is Samorobin. In Cyrillic Russian the word is derived from two separate words, Samo, meaning self and Robin, operator. The fact that we are told this self operating machine is one hundred leagues above the earth, which corresponds with the 400 kilometre high orbit of the MIR space station, seems to clarify the fact that he is talking about a satellite. His use of Cyrillic Russian may even give us a further clue as to the identity of the satellite and its country of origin. The most worrying part of this quatrain is the first line. What kind of pestilent wave could possibly cause a great famine. Is Nostradamus in some way trying to tell us that this pestilent wave, perhaps radioactivity, is caused by a satellite, perhaps a nuclear powered satellite re-entering earth's atmosphere and leaving a cloud of radioactive dust over the northern hemisphere. The fact that the word "Samorobin" brings this quatrain into the latter half of this century seems rather worrying. One thing does appear to be clear however, as the MIR space station descends into the atmosphere and begins to burn up it will be seen around the world, perhaps another sign in the sky.

And when these things begin to come to pass, then look up, and lift up your heads; for your redemption draweth nigh.

St. Luke 21. Verse 28

What the effects of these celestial events will have on the planet, the population and our future are of course uncertain. Whether they are portents of disasters and calamities to come remains to be seen. However one thing is certain.........
we will know soon..

Chapter 7
Signs of the Times.

O ye hypocrites, ye can discern the face of the sky;
but can ye not discern the signs of the times.
Matthew 16. verse 3

One of the most interesting things about ancient prophecy is that previous attempts to correctly interpret prophecies have failed because the time was not right. Until the latter part of the twentieth century many of the events described in the prophecies had not occurred. Israel only became a nation in 1948. The Israelis did not recapture East Jerusalem and the Temple Mount until 1967. Global warming, rising sea levels, nuclear power, space flight and many other events and innovations have only recently come about and been understood as we reached the end of the twentieth century. This is the reason why many previous interpretations of prophecy have been incorrect. It would appear that the major apocalyptic prophecies were meant to be understood only when the time was right. In other words when the signs given by the prophets could be seen and understood on earth, then the time was approaching. Look around you and you will see that everywhere there are signs of the times.

Economically, environmentally and politically it seems the world has now reached "the latter days" spoken of by Daniel. We have developed the capacity to destroy the world and it's population by war, famine, plague, environmental catastrophe and evil. The four horsemen of the Apocalypse, representing plague, famine, war and conquest are with us now. The problems the world will experience over the next few years will create a situation tailor made for the rise of the antichrist.

As I discussed in Chapter 3, the concept of the antichrist as a single person who appears on the world stage may not be as straightforward as it appears. Indeed, the number 666, the number of the Beast, appears to signify not a single person, but mankind as a whole, playing God, deciding on the fate of nations and individuals and thus forming an un-holy trinity.

However, the idea of one single person being the catalyst of our destruction cannot be dismissed. Nor that of a single belief, religion or political ideology causing the same trouble. Look at the many problems various cults and sects have caused over the years, their leaders claiming divine guidance only to consign their followers to a tragic death.

> *For false Christs and prophets shall rise, and shall show signs and wonders, to seduce, if it were possible, even the elect.*
>
> Mark 13. verse 22

Look around at the political leaders who occupy the world stage at the moment and consider the power that rests in their hands. Their decisions, made in consultation with the heads of global multinational companies, can consign a third world economy to the scrap heap, its people to revolution, famine, starvation and death. One should not forget that though it is the people who fight wars, it is the politicians who start them. Recently we have seen a great deal of unrest within certain quarters concerning the role of the International Monetary Fund and the World Bank in the economic affairs of the third world. The perception amongst many people is that the loans provided by the aforementioned institutions come with such restrictive conditions that, rather than helping third world countries, they are in fact shouldering them with such crippling burdens of debt that the people of these countries are destined to remain in abject poverty for the foreseeable future. The fact that it is the wealthy countries of the world who are saddling the third world with these enormous debts only adds to the perception of many that the International Monetary Fund and the World Bank, together with the World Trade Organisation, are instruments of a capitalist ideology bent on enslaving the third world for many years to come. Where once guns and bombs where the instruments of warfare; money, power and wealth are the new weapons of conflict. In an analogy of the now famous "chaos" theory, it could be said that for every dollar of debt interest paid to the developed world, a child in the third world dies. This is a situation which is morally unjustifiable and, according to Nostradamus, is doomed to failure.

Des Royes et princes dresseront simulachres,
Augures, creux eslevez aruspices;
Corne victime doree, et d'azur, d'acres
Interpretez seront les exstipices.

They will fabricate images of Kings and princes,
Prophets/Soothsayers, will make hollow promises;
The horn of plenty will fall victim to them, and peace will turn to violence
The prophecies will be fulfilled.

Century 3. Quatrain 26

In this remarkable quatrain similes paint a fascinating picture of the use of money and the eventual consequences of the political ineptitude of our world leaders. The images of Kings and princes refers directly to the world currencies and the engraving of the heads of state on coins. The prophets or soothsayers are politicians and world leaders. In line three the word "Corne" refers to Cornucopia, the horn of plenty, quite literally the consumer society. It appears that Nostradamus envisages the collapse of our financial systems brought about by world politicians and resulting in war. A parallel can be made with the economic experience of Germany in the 1930's, however, this problem appears to be world wide. In a similar quatrain Nostradamus once again uses the same symbolism and seems to refer to the enormous debt that the third world is now experiencing.

Les simulachres d'or et d'argent enflez,
Qu'apres le rapt lac au feu furent jettez,
Au descouvert estaincts tous et troublez,
Au marbre escripts, perscripts interjettez.

The images of gold and silver inflated,
Which after the theft of prosperity will be thrown
into the fire in anger,
At the discovery the debt is exhausted and
dissipated,
The scripts and bonds will be pulped.

Century 8. Quatrain 28

Once again the images of gold and silver refer to money. In line two the word "lac" refers to the milk of human kindness, quite literally prosperity. The word "marbre" in line four symbolises a marble pestle and mortar used for crushing or pulping. It would seem that once again Nostradamus envisages world wide inflation and the collapse of our economic and financial systems. There will be many people who doubt that the world's economies could possibly collapse, citing the strength of the U.S. economy as proof of this. However, Dr. J.S.Chiappalone, MD, has this to say in his essay Terminal Madness of the Endtime :-

"The US is unofficially bankrupt and the economy a bubble of spuriousness, built on false hope, which is about to burst. Warnings by financial archons such as Alan Greenspan and others have been ignored with the hubris of minds self-satisfied in the efficacy of their own illusion".

What event exactly brings about this world wide economic collapse is unclear, but in Chapter Three, The Beast, I make mention that the Bible seems to predict a world wide currency, the beginnings of which can be seen in Europe right now.

And that no man might buy or sell, save he that had the mark, or the name of the beast or the number of his name.
Revelation 13. verse 17

This verse immediately precedes the famous final verse of Revelation 13 in which the number 666 is mentioned, and could once again allude to the fact that The Beast, or Antichrist, is not just a single person, but mankind itself using the ideology of finance, commerce and money to control not just the Nations, States and Countries of the world, but individual people, you and me. Look around at the world today and consider the huge financial power and control that the "so-called" G7 countries of the industrialised nations hold over the vast majority of the worlds' population. The poorer nations continue to go cap in hand to them for aid, but the restrictions placed on these loans is prohibitive and continues the downward spiral into poverty that some eighty percent of the worlds population now experiences.

That man should have made himself so greedy and should have so wholly deluded himself and have failed to realise that his days must needs thereby be shortened".
Preface to the Prognostications of Paracelsus

Not only does the Preface to the Prognostications seem to mirror the economic situation in the world today, but further on in the Preface, Paracelsus draws a distinct parallel with the problems this is causing in the world.

It is also a subject for contemplation in what manner the people on earth inflict misery on each other, whereby no one will grant his fellow that the sun shall shine upon him.
Preface to the Prognostications of Paracelsus

Perhaps one of the best examples of the problems the world is facing at this present time is to be seen in Africa. Not only is this great continent racked by civil wars and regional unrest, with armed conflict, poverty and starvation stalking the land, but AIDS, the great scourge of the world has now reached pandemic proportions across most of the continent, condemning millions to a slow lingering death and leaving many regions populated only by orphans. Slowly the world is waking up and acknowledging the problems faced by Africa, but it seems a lack of political will and an indifferent attitude from the worlds rich countries and nations is condemning Africa to years of starvation, death, war and famine.

> *Thus he said, The fourth beast shall be the fourth kingdom upon earth, which shall be diverse from all kingdoms, and shall devour the whole earth, and shall tread it down, and break it in pieces.*
> Daniel 7. verse 23

Consider, then, the implications of a global currency dominating the world, holding all the nations and peoples in it's power, that suddenly collapses, and the effect this would have on the third world, let alone the rich nations. Events that are beyond our control, natural disasters in particular, can destabilise the worlds financial markets overnight. The advent of Information Technology and the rapid improvements in telecommunications mean that the World's economies, finances and currencies are now traded globally through electronic communications, computers, telephone lines and the internet. And as we have seen recently, these global systems can be hacked into, details changed, information accessed, security breached and systems crashed. It is quite possible that a Cyber-terrorist could manipulate the financial markets and cause a global economic collapse.

I recently received an e-mail describing in a somewhat convoluted way how the number **666** could be interpreted as the **www** that precedes internet addresses. At first this idea may seem fanciful, but it is certainly a fact that more and more of our lives are being controlled by computers, telecommunications and the internet. There is also something to be said for the argument that the internet is the final step in the globalisation of the world. Business, commerce and finance are no longer confined by their countries of origin, they have integrated, merged and metamorphosed into global enterprises that hold such huge sway over the people of the planet that even governments must consult with them before decisions are made. The tool that has perhaps, more than any other, allowed this globalisation to take place is the internet. Developed from American surveillance satellites the internet now allows people to communicate as never before in our history. Decisions made anywhere in the world are simultaneously understood and available across the globe via the world wide web. As we have seen in both the Gulf war and latterly NATO's bombing of Serbia, wars can also be fought using the internet not only as a tool for communication and instruction, but to control the placement of the laser guided bombs used during these campaigns. There are those who say that the next war will be fought over the internet with generals guiding their machines of battle from thousands of miles away, cocooned, isolated and desensitised from the mayhem they are creating. Whether the antichrist is mankind as a whole or a single individual, the world wide web provides enormous opportunities for propaganda, disinformation, control and subversion on a scale hitherto unthought of. Looked at in this light, the correlation between the number **666** and the **www** of internet addresses is not perhaps as far fetched as one might imagine.

Should the antichrist turn out to be a single person it is to be presumed this person would also use all the tools at his disposal, including the internet, to cause the problems that appear to be being prepared for an unsuspecting world.

Nostradamus appears to identify the antichrist as a person from the East.

> *Tant attendu ne reviendra jamais*
> *Dedans l'Europe, en Asie apparoistra*
> *Un de la ligue islu du grand Hermes,*
> *Et sur tous rois des orientz croistra.*

Long awaited he will never return in Europe,
in Asia he will appear
One of the league issued from the great Hermes,
and he will have power above all the kings of the
East.

Century 10. Quatrain 75

In Chapter 2, Judgement Day, I give an explanation of this quatrain. It is difficult to speculate on the identity that Nostradamus is giving, other than to suggest that there are many people in the Middle East and Asia who would wish to see their own particular ideologies pre-eminent in the world. The problems and difficulties between Jews and Moslems over the sanctity of East Jerusalem and the Temple Mount, or Haram al Sharif, The Noble Sanctuary, as Moslem's call it, and who shall control this area, the third holiest shrine of Islam, seems, even after years of debate, to be an insoluble problem that could quite easily start another war in the Middle East, the consequences of which would go beyond that countries borders. There are problems too with the way that the sparse water supplies of Palestine are distributed between Moslems and Jews, consigning some to a serious lack of water, whilst others have plenty. However, perhaps the main weapon the countries of the Middle East and Persia can use against the developed world is oil. Over the last thirty years the western world has seen the power that these countries can exert on a consumer society that seems unable to satiate it's greed for petroleum. Here once again is another weapon that can be used to destroy economies, and as was seen during the Gulf War, the western world would, if deprived of its petroleum, use any power within its grasp to restore its supplies of oil. It has done so before, it will do it again.

So far in this chapter I have discussed whether or not the antichrist is a single person or a single ideology promulgated by mankind. That either of these could be the catalyst of a world wide catastrophe is, I believe, without question. There is, however, another serious threat to the future of mankind that we can do nothing about. I have already discussed natural events such as earthquakes and volcanic eruptions in previous chapters and will do so again in the next. Whilst the power of these events do indeed pose a threat to mankind, scientists have recently discovered an even more cataclysmic scenario that we are only just becoming aware of. These are called Near Earth Objects.

And the second angel sounded, and as it were a great mountain burning with fire was cast into the sea, and the third part of the sea became blood.
Revelation 8. verse 8

The discovery of these objects over the last few years has led many astronomers to call for a concerted international effort to identify asteroids and comets whose orbits could, in the future, cross earth's path and collide with the planet. The effects of any cosmic collision with earth would be catastrophic, and scientists and astronomers have recently found evidence of past collisions that have caused enormous damage. The problem with these near earth objects is that scientists and astronomers are not aware of their closeness to earth until it's almost too late. On Friday 1st. September 2000 the 2000 QW7 asteroid, which originated in the asteroid belt between Mars and Jupiter, passed within 2.4 million miles of the earth. In cosmic terms this was a near miss. A scientist equated it's closeness to earth as being comparable to a man at one end of a tennis court throwing a marble at a man at the other end of the court and missing his head by the width of a hand. The worrying fact is that the asteroids approach was detected by Cornell University only six days before it hurtled past earth.

The evidence of damage caused by objects impacting with the earth is now widely known and accepted. Some 65 million years ago an asteroid seven miles wide hit the Yucatan peninsula and formed the Gulf of Mexico. It also caused the extinction of the dinosaurs and three quarters of all the living species on the planet. In 1908, an asteroid about 60 metres wide landed at Tunguska in Siberia flattening trees over a thirteen mile area and killing hundreds of reindeer. If the asteroid had landed in New York the city would have been completely destroyed killing millions. Scientists say that if 2000 QW7, which is nine times larger than the Tunguska asteroid, had impacted in the Atlantic Ocean, everything within two miles would have been vaporised and the East Coast of the United States and the West Coast of Europe would have been swept by massive tidal waves. Molten debris would rain down for weeks after the impact, and dust particles thrown up into the atmosphere would block out the sun and have the same effects as a nuclear winter. Nothing would grow, the earth would starve.

> But in those days, after that tribulation, the sun shall be darkened, and the moon shall not give her light.

> Mark 13. verse 24

Evidence of a similar event has recently been uncovered by scientists studying ice cores from the Greenland icecap and tree rings from Oak trees preserved and recovered from Irish peat bogs. Dr. Mike Baillie of Queens University, Belfast has discovered what appears to have been an asteroid or comet strike on the earth about 540 AD. The dendrochronology and ice core samples of the time show that earth suffered many years of little or no sunlight, resulting in agriculture being devastated and malnutrition and starvation running rampant, the consequent famine and the plague that accompanied this event killing millions. These were, quite literally, the dark ages.

There shall come times of dark affliction
Of scarcity, of sorrow, and of wailing;
In the latter ages of the world's existence.
The Prophecies of St Columbkille verse 6

It is interesting to note that both the ancient Egyptian and the Mayan civilisations predict that the earth and its population will suffer major problems and unrest which seemingly start at the beginning of this new millennium. The Great Pyramid of Cheops has been studied by archaeologists, scientists, academics and Egyptologists for thousands of years with some remarkable conclusions. The passages and chambers within the Pyramid appear to represent a timescale that some commentators believe gives a clear set of datings for events in the future. Amongst those who have written at length on this matter are Morton Edgar and Max Toth, both of whom use measurements devised by John Davidson to date the chambers in the Pyramid.

The conclusion they have reached involves the Great Subterranean Chamber in Cheops, and what most archaeologists call the "Pit of Ordeal" or the "Pit of Destruction". Though datings are a little imprecise, about + or - 3 years, there can be no doubting that by using Davidson's method of measurement, namely one primitive inch equals one year, the dates 1914 and 1939, representing World Wars 1 and 2 are clearly indicated, and using the same method, the Great Subterranean Passage enters the "Pit of Destruction" in 2003 and seems to last some twenty years before coming to a dead end.

The Mayan civilisation, now proved to be closely connected with the Egyptians, also appears to give a dating for what seems to be a major catastrophe on earth. Archaeologists are unsure if this dating pertains to the end of the world, or to an event that is the precursor of the end time. The date, however, is extremely precise. December 24th. 2013. Many readers will find these datings spurious, but they are well publicised and have one thing in common which is undeniable. They point to a major world wide calamity at the beginning of the new millennium

For then shall be great tribulation, such as was not since the beginning of the world to this time, no, nor ever shall be.

Mathew 24. verse 21

The fact that prophecy can, in many cases, only be seen to be correct after the event, prompts many people to be cynical about talk of the "end times." However, recently the veracity of prophecy was endorsed by no less a person than the Holy Father himself. Speaking about the famous prophecies of Fatima, in Portugal, John Paul II conceded that the vision of a priest in white falling to the ground, part of the final Fatima prophecy, was true and represented the assassination attempt on him on the 13th. May 1981. It is interesting to note, however, that the full text of the final Fatima prophecy has never been published, and there are those who have investigated the Fatima prophecies who claim that the priest in white is, in fact, killed, not wounded, and this event triggers the tribulations spoken of in the book of Mathew. Whatever the truth of the matter, it seems that many of the ancient prophecies point to a time of trouble starting at the beginning of this, the new millennium. Take a look around at the world at the present moment and it is clear that there are many threats to the stability of the planet, both man made and natural, but it is the natural catastrophes that we have no control over, and the consequences of a major natural event could well bring about the "tribulations" that the Bible and other prophecies talk about.

*And the third angel sounded, and there fell a great
star out of heaven, burning as it were a lamp, and
it fell upon the third part of the rivers and upon the
fountains of waters;
And the name of the star is called Wormwood: and
a third part of the waters became wormwood; and
many men died of the waters, because they were
made bitter.*

Revelation 8. verses 10 and 11

Perhaps the most interesting part of these two verses is the
use of the name Wormwood. Wormwood is a bitter herb used
primarily in the making of the drink Absinthe. However, the
name Wormwood translates into Cyrillic Russian as
"Chernobyl". On 26th. April 1986 the nuclear power plant at
Chernobyl in the Ukraine exploded, causing a massive
release of radiation into the atmosphere that polluted vast
areas of Russia and Europe. Fourteen years later the death
toll from this terrible accident is claimed to be forty thousand,
with many still dying from the effects of radiation poisoning.
The star that St. John describes falling from heaven appears
to pollute the waters and rivers. Is this a description of a
nuclear missile falling to earth, or is this a reference once
again to a comet or asteroid colliding with the planet?
Governments, politicians and scientists are now starting to
realise that a collision between an asteroid or comet and the
planet would destroy us. In a rare show of international
co-operation, world leaders, environmentalists and scientists
agree that some form of defence against objects striking
earth has to be put in place. Most talk about the use of a
nuclear warhead launched at the incoming object and
exploded alongside or in front of the object, thus knocking it
out of it's trajectory and hopefully away from the earth.
Science of this kind is extremely hazardous and seems very
open to a law which is never taken as seriously as perhaps it
should be. Sod's law says "If it can go wrong, it will". Any kind
of nuclear missile strike launched against an incoming object
would have a limited chance of success and could cause

more damage to the earth than we expect. If, for instance, the nuclear explosion fragmented the incoming asteroid the earth could well be hit by multiple particles of rock, causing more destruction than a single strike.

And there fell upon men a great hail out of heaven, every stone about the weight of a talent; and men blasphemed God because of the plague of hail, for the plague thereof was exceeding great.
Revelation 16. verse 21

It is also interesting to note that a thermonuclear explosion generates a huge electronic pulse radiating outwards for many miles. One of the known consequences of this pulse is that it disables anything electrical or digital in it's path. The internet, telecommunications, economic and financial transactions all depend on satellites to facilitate their business. A nuclear explosion in space would disable these satellites, and bring business around the world to a halt. The fact that this project is expected to take between six and ten years to set up may also be leaving things a little too late. Astronomers now point to the fact that earth is long overdue a major asteroid, comet or meteor strike.

And a mighty angel took up a stone like a great millstone, and cast it into the sea, saying, Thus with violence shall that great city Babylon be thrown down, and shall be found no more at all.
Revelation 18. verse 21

Scientists searching for near earth objects that could strike the planet are all of one accord with regard to their research. It is almost impossible to locate every threat to earth amongst the thousands of asteroids and other objects moving around the solar system. As telescopes become more powerful and the search for near earth objects gains momentum it may be possible to detect certain asteroids and comets whose orbits will bring them into close proximity with us, the problem however is not the identification of these objects, but what to do about them in the short time we will have before they hit earth.

The conclusions regarding the question of whether it is a single person, a single ideology or a natural catastrophe that causes the problems that appear to be approaching us remain difficult to establish. However, it would seem foolish not to take prophecy seriously, as we could be dismissing what may be our future. Look around at the signs the world is being shown now and it seems that they are indeed "signs of the times". It also seems that time is now.

Chapter 8
Nemesis

"Behold it, you scorners, and wonder at it, and vanish away, because I am working a work in your days, a work that you will by no means believe even if anyone relates it to you in detail."

Acts 13. verse 41

To most people the idea that the world as we know it could cease to exist in their own lifetime is risible. Most scoff at the idea that our brave, new, technological world could ever come to an end. Perhaps the reason for this attitude stems from a falling away of peoples belief in God. Pascal, the French mathematician and philosopher had an astute view on this when he said:

"If you do not believe in God, and he exists, you have a problem. If you believe in God and he does not exist, no problem."

Those who do not believe in God, naturally do not believe The Bible, and therefore give no credence to the prophecies contained therein. Similarly, the other books of ancient prophecy, from The Book of Enoch through to Nostradamus, are seen in the same light, and are not believed. In my opinion, this is sheer folly.

For when they shall say, Peace and safety; then sudden destruction cometh upon them, as travail upon a woman with child; and they shall not escape.

1 Thessalonians 5. verse 3

As we enter a brand new millennium, it is well that we should reflect on the damage, horrors and carnage that mankind has unleashed on this planet and it's inhabitants over the final century of the last millennium. Two World Wars, the Russian

Revolution, The Great Leap Forward - Hitler, Stalin and Mao between them responsible for the deaths of over one hundred million people. Now, as we stand poised on the edge of a new era, look around you and see if we have learned the lessons of the past. Look at Africa, The Balkans, Indonesia and The Caucasus.

Look too at the climatic and environmental legacy of the twentieth century. Increasing holes in the ozone layer, global warming leading to climatic change that can already be seen around us. Massive flooding, storms, hurricanes and tornadoes wreaking havoc on an unprecedented scale. Sea levels rising, threatening entire nations. Skin cancers reaching epidemic proportions. World food supplies threatened by drought. This is no doomsday scenario, this is happening now.

Pollution of our rivers and oceans, a legacy of the industrial revolution of the 19th. Century, continues unabated, with the amount of toxic and nuclear waste dumped into the seas ever increasing, despite the certain knowledge that we are killing all who live there, and in so doing depriving ourselves of yet more food. Some of the great rivers of the world are now dead, devoid of any life, unfit for humans to bathe in. Look at the Danube.

We create and genetically engineer our food, our animals and our babies, whilst at the same time inventing monstrous chemical and biological weapons that can wipe out the entire population of the planet. The arms industries of the world continue to manufacture and supply weapons of frightening power to anyone, friend or foe, prepared to buy them, whilst dictators and tyrants amass billion dollar fortunes as their people starve on the streets. And all the time, first world countries prosper and grow wealthier to the detriment of a poverty stricken and starving third world. This is a recipe for disaster.

Racism, bigotry, hatred, nationalism and persecution are the new buzz words of the twenty first century. That grand illusion of the late sixties, love, peace, understanding and a better world have now been replaced forever by the insular, protectionist, selfish and greedy "me" society that eventually spawns suspicion and distrust and leads inevitably to ethnic cleansing and war. This is not a legacy from some dim and distant time long forgotten, it is policy practised now by politicians, rulers, despots and megalomaniacs alike, blinded by ambition, power and money who, rather than admit to their own corruption, dishonesty and failure would prefer to start wars, even among their own people. It has happened in the past. It is happening now.

The ever increasing rate of natural disasters occurring around the globe could not have come at a worse time. As global warming increases and the climate continues to change at an alarming rate, the consequences of natural phenomena like earthquakes and volcanic eruptions around the planet will only serve to worsen a world wide situation that is clearly getting out of hand. Nobody, it seems, except a handful of environmentalists, appear to see the global implications of catastrophic events over which we have no control.

> *Behold, the Lord maketh the earth empty, and maketh it waste, and turneth it upside down, and scattereth abroad the inhabitants thereof.*
> *The earth shall reel to and fro like a drunkard, and shall be removed like a cottage; and the transgression thereof shall be heavy upon it; and it shall fall, and not rise again*
> Isaiah 24. verses1 and 20

The most destructive forces on the planet are not man-made but natural. A volcanic eruption can release a great deal more energy than the worlds entire nuclear arsenal, as can a major earthquake. Over the last few years we have seen the incredible destruction that can be caused by earthquakes and volcanoes, as well as hurricanes, typhoons and tropical storms, initiating flooding on a Biblical scale, and leaving the inhabitants of these areas without homes, food and the basic essentials for life.

Recently a major discovery was made regarding the danger volcanic eruptions can pose to entire continents by precipitating what are called "Mega Tsunamis." Scientists now realise that, in the near future, it is quite possible that a giant wave of water that would swamp the Caribbean and much of the eastern seaboard of the United States, could be released by a collapsing volcano thousands of miles away.

Dr Simon Day , who works at the Benfield Greig Hazards Research Centre, University College London, suggests that one flank of the Cumbre Vieja volcano on the island of La Palma, in the Canaries, is unstable and could plunge into the ocean. He adds this warning, published in the New Scientist on 7th. October 2000. "If the volcano collapsed in one block (almost 20 cubic kilometres of rock) it would fall into water 6km deep and create a wave 650 metres tall. This would travel across the Atlantic at about 720kph. The wave would weaken only slightly as it crossed the ocean, and would probably be 40-50 metres high by the time it made landfall. The surge would create havoc as much as 20 kilometres inland".

Scientists are now in agreement with many of the once vilified "doom merchants" of Greenpeace and Friends of the Earth in admitting that "global warming" does exist, greenhouse gasses are having a serious affect on the planets ecological systems, the ice-caps are melting , water levels are rising, the hydrological system of the planet is in a state of flux and climate change is accelerating at such an alarming rate that some say that within the next ten years we will be unable to sustain food production in the Western world. We are in deep trouble.

"But the day of the Lord will come as a thief in the night; in which the heavens shall pass away with a great noise, and the elements shall melt with fervent heat, the earth also and the works therein shall be burned up."

2 Peter 3. verse 10

An English scientist who has worked for many years with the National Aeronautical and Space Administration, Professor James Lovelock, came up with one of the most interesting and startling theories concerning the problems that the world now appears to be facing. It is called the Gaia hypothesis.

The Gaia hypothesis contends that the planet functions as a single organism that regulates itself. The living creatures within this living organism that is earth, including human beings, change the environment as well as adapting to it. But if those changes are adverse, the planet will rid itself of whatever is causing the harm. Now look around you at the damage that mankind has inflicted on the earth over the last century, and the problems that are now confronting us. The implications of the Gaia hypothesis are only too obvious. Mankind has fought against nature and the planet. It is now the turn of the planet to fight back. Whatever we may consider ourselves to be, however technologically advanced we think we are and no matter how mentally superior to all other forms of life we appear, mankind cannot fight against nature. It is the most powerful force on earth. It will destroy us.

We have sown the wind, and now we must reap the whirlwind. We have spent the last three decades of the twentieth century breeding the inheritors of an environmental Armageddon and the cannon fodder for World War III. It would seem that mankind has not learned the lessons of the past, but has continued on a course that can have only one possible conclusion. If the planet does not destroy us, we will destroy ourselves.

Conclusion

For these be the days of vengeance, that all things which are written may be fulfilled.

Luke 21. Verse 22

Over the preceding few chapters I have attempted to give the reader a dispassionate and subjective comparison between ancient prophecy and events that are now unfolding on earth. Over the last century man has become the most destructive force on earth, threatening the entire human race with extinction. The events of the last few years in the former Yugoslavia, Rwanda, the Gulf, Zaire and many other areas of the world prove that despite the horrors of two world wars last century, man's inhumanity to his fellow man continues unabated .

At the same time, man continues his reckless pollution of the rivers, seas, oceans and atmosphere of the planet, threatening the global ecosystem with collapse and the consequent world wide famine that would result.

Natural disasters are of course almost impossible to predict, but the results can be as devastating as any war. Recently a phenomenon known as El Niño, Spanish for the Baby Jesus, appeared in the southern Pacific Ocean. At certain times for no known scientific reason, the waters of the southern Pacific rise in temperature. Scientists studying El Niño announced in June 1997 that they had detected the greatest climatic disturbance for 50 years, the sea temperature having risen at a faster rate than ever recorded before. Scientist say that the influence of El Niño and its sister in the northern Pacific, La Niña, on the global climate has been significant during the last few years, causing droughts, storms and high winds around the world. Indeed some say that the trade winds and ocean currents in the southern Pacific could reverse causing havoc for global weather patterns. Just what effect this climatic upheaval may have on the food producing areas of the world is impossible to predict, but Nostradamus has a frightening view of the way the world is heading.

La grande famine que je sens aprocher,
Souvent tourner, puis estre universelle:
Si grande & long qu'un viendra arracher,
Du bois racine & l'enfant de mamelle.

The great famine that I sense approaching
Will turn, then will become universal:
It will be so great and long lasting they will
dig up the roots of trees and grab children from the breast.

Century 1. Quatrain 67

It is currently estimated that there are one billion people on the planet who don't have enough to eat. The scenario that Nostradamus describes in this quatrain reflects the situation that exists today. He says the famine "will turn" indicating it will occur in various parts of the world before it eventually becomes world wide. The last two lines indicate the desperation of the population as they try to feed themselves, and in the last line Nostradamus seems to hint at cannibalism. It is a fact that during the conflict in former Yugoslavia starving people ate the bodies of dead children.

La voix ouie de l'insolite oiseau,
Sur le canon de respiral etage:
Si hault viendra du froment le boisseau,
Que l'homme d'homme sera Antropophage.

The call of the unwanted bird will be heard,
On the pipe of the breathing floor:
So high will be the price of bushels of wheat
That man will eat his fellow man.

Century 2. Quatrain 75

The first two lines of this quatrain are at first, somewhat strange. The unwanted bird symbolises a bird of ill-omen and line two is Nostradamus' description of a chimney stack. A bird of ill omen on a chimney stack denotes famine and bad times. Lines three and four are self explanatory, the word "antropophage" coming from the Greek "tropophage" meaning "man eating". What causes this world wide famine is unclear, but it is now clear from scientific evidence that global warming, together with natural occurrences such as El Niño and volcanic eruptions can have a disastrous effect on world climate.

Brent Blackwelder, the American Chairman of Friends of the Earth said recently in a television documentary, "Global warming is affecting everything that lives and breathes upon the planet. Severe storms, hurricanes, tornadoes, huge amounts of rainfall, floods... some nations will entirely disappear. This is what is going to confront us, worse than we imagine".

A team of British scientists led by Bill McGuire, professor of geological hazards at University College London, has found that the rise in sea levels caused by global warming could trigger off major volcanic eruptions. The team observed that 90% of volcanoes are close to or surrounded by sea. As water rises it erodes the lava. Eventually the mountain becomes unable to withstand the internal pressure of the molten rock and explodes. They predict the rise in volcanic activity may damage cities, have a catastrophic affect on world climate and damage air quality so badly that millions could die from respiratory ailments.

Sir John Houghton, co-chairman of the United Nations Intergovernmental Panel on Climate Change speaking on the affects of rising sea levels caused by global warming says, "floods and droughts will occur in different parts of the world due to changes in the hydrological cycle. All the models we have produce the same robust result and to say nothing will happen is quite simply unreal".

The effects of a world wide famine whatever the cause, are simply too frightening to contemplate. How would the almost six billion people who live on this planet react? What would the politicians and world leaders do? Would the world's population just lie down and die? These are questions people should ponder.

Questions should also be asked about the consequences of a collapse in the world economy. The earthquake predicted by Nostradamus in Century nine, quatrain 83 and discussed in Chapter four appears to predict what the Californians call "the big one". The San Andreas fault is the most studied fault line on the planet. It runs down California and is where the Pacific tectonic plate meets the American plate. The Pacific plate is enormous running as it does down the coast of America, South America, across the Pacific and upwards through New Zealand, Japan and the Kuril Islands, along the so called "ring of fire".

Scientists studying the San Andreas fault say that the "big one" when it occurs could be of such force that the entire Pacific plate may move causing massive earthquakes along its perimeter. Not only would California be devastated but Japan, a country notorious for its earthquakes, could quite literally be cut in half. If California were a country, it would be the fifth wealthiest country in the world, Japan is, after America the second wealthiest nation in the world. Should an earthquake devastate both California and Japan the consequences to the world's financial markets would be apocalyptic. Stock markets around the world would crash, banks and insurance companies, major investors in both California and Japan would become insolvent and peoples investments and savings would be wiped out. In short, the world's economy would collapse and scientists studying the San Andreas fault are all in accord about the "big one". It will occur, the only question is when?

That mankind may be responsible for these disasters, that mankind through his greed will cause the climatic changes and world wide disruption that global warming will bring is described in the Old Testament book of Isaiah.

The earth also is defiled under the inhabitants thereof; because they have transgressed the laws, changed the ordinance, broken the everlasting covenant.
Therefore hath the curse devoured the earth, and they that dwell therein are desolate: therefore the inhabitants of the earth are burned, and few men left.

Isaiah 24. verses 5 and 6

These two verses not only mirror the preceding prophecies of Nostradamus, but also the predictions of the Book of Revelation Chapter 16, discussed in Chapter four of this book.

Consider then the situation the world finds itself in at the moment. Almost one fifth of the world's population are hungry, there are currently over 80 wars being fought around the globe, terrorism is on the increase and the threat of global war moves inexorably closer, the worlds economies are in increasing turmoil and the world's ecosystem is being destroyed. It seems that mankind's actions are beginning to bring about the global catastrophes predicted in the ancient prophecies and in doing so will precipitate the prophecy of Jesus Christ.

For then shall be great tribulation, such as was not since the beginning of the world to this time, no, nor ever shall be.
And except those days should be shortened, there should no flesh be saved: but for the elects sake those days shall be shortened.

Matthew 24. verses 21 and 22

What then is going to happen between now and 2023? Will the predictions and prophecies contained in this book come to fruition? Some I know will be sceptical, others disbelieving and others perhaps afraid. To them and to those who do believe I can only finish by using the words of Jesus Christ.

And what I say unto you I say unto all, watch.
Mark 13. verse 37.

THE END

I should to thank the many librarians and libraries throughout the world, as well as the many other learned people, too numerous to mention, who helped me during my research for this book

Ian Gurney.
May 1999.